# Human Resource Management and Evolutionary Psychology

# ELGAR FOOTPRINTS IN HUMAN RESOURCE MANAGEMENT AND EMPLOYMENT RELATIONS

**Series Editors:** Tony Dundon, *Professor of HRM and Employment Relations, Work and Employment Studies, Kemmy Business School, University of Limerick, Ireland and Visiting Professor, Work and Equalities Institute, University of Manchester, UK*, Adrian Wilkinson, *Professor of Employment Relations, Griffith University, Australia* and Maike Andresen, *Chair of Human Resource Management, University of Bamberg, Germany*

We are proud to introduce a new series of short books defining the future of human resource management and employment relations research. Leading thinkers are given the space and creative freedom to build on their contribution to the field in new ways. *Footprints* give the reader a concise, innovative and 'must-read, must-cite' take on research and thematic debates.

Led by three distinguished scholars, Adrian Wilkinson, Tony Dundon and Maike Andresen, and quicker to market than the journals process, this high quality, exclusive series seeks to publish a limited number of key volumes per year to advance discussion within human resource management and employment relations.

Offering an alternative method of academic dialogue, these books will be more in depth than a journal article, shorter than a standard book, refreshing to read, thematically-led and debating polemic arguments in the field – a new platform for future research in a particular sub-field for both new and established academics.

Titles in the series include:

Human Resource Management and Evolutionary Psychology
Exploring the Biological Foundations of Managing People at Work
*Andrew R. Timming*

# Human Resource Management and Evolutionary Psychology

Exploring the Biological Foundations of Managing People at Work

Andrew R. Timming, Ph.D.

*Associate Professor of Human Resource Management, University of Western Australia Business School, Australia*

ELGAR FOOTPRINTS IN HUMAN RESOURCE MANAGEMENT AND EMPLOYMENT RELATIONS

Edward Elgar
PUBLISHING

Cheltenham, UK • Northampton, MA, USA

Published by
Edward Elgar Publishing Limited
The Lypiatts
15 Lansdown Road
Cheltenham
Glos GL50 2JA
UK

Edward Elgar Publishing, Inc.
William Pratt House
9 Dewey Court
Northampton
Massachusetts 01060
USA

A catalogue record for this book
is available from the British Library

Library of Congress Control Number: 2019935394

This book is available electronically in the **Elgar**online
Business subject collection
DOI 10.4337/9781788977913

ISBN 978 1 78897 790 6 (cased)
ISBN 978 1 78897 791 3 (eBook)

Typeset by Servis Filmsetting Ltd, Stockport, Cheshire
Printed and bound in Great Britain by TJ International Ltd, Padstow, Cornwall

For Oliver, Ailsa, and, of course, for Wing

# Contents

# About the author

Andrew R. Timming is Associate Professor of Human Resource Management at the University of Western Australia Business School. He holds a Ph.D. from the University of Cambridge, England. He draws from the theory and methods of organizational, experimental, and evolutionary psychology and economic sociology in his writings. His research centers mainly around personnel selection and assessment, employee participation and involvement in decision-making, and workplace bullying and health. He is an Associate Editor at both *Human Resource Management Journal* and *International Journal of Human Resource Management*. He also serves as the Director of Business and Community Engagement in the Department of Management & Organizations at the University of Western Australia Business School.

# Acknowledgements

No one writes a book on one's own. This one, certainly, is the product of a myriad of discussions I've had with friends and colleagues over the years. As Isaac Newton once said, "If I have seen further it is by standing on the shoulders of Giants." I want to thank my colleagues at the University of Western Australia for discussions that have helped to shape the arguments presented in this book, and indeed my thanks also go out to the University itself for providing me with a stimulating environment in which to write it. I also want to thank Ben Jones, Lisa DeBruine, and David Perrett for, through their own research, helping me to better understand the evolutionary foundations of this book, as well as Dennis Nickson and Chris Warhurst for their pioneering work on aesthetic labor. The editorial staff at Edward Elgar have been very helpful and responsive, and to them I also send my thanks. I want to thank Man Wing Timming, my wife and my best friend, for helping me to organize the chapters into a coherent whole, and for putting up with me more generally. The same goes for my children. And what kind of man could forget to thank his parents and siblings? Mom, Dad, Justin, Josh, Meghan, and Marcus, I love you all.

Andrew R. Timming
Perth, Australia
2018

# 1. The evolutionary psychology of human resource management

Human resource management, as both an academic field of study and a set of professional practices, stands on the precipice of obsolescence (Dundon and Rafferty, 2018). Although its "modern" origins can be traced back to the early 1980s (see Beer et al., 1984), the discipline today appears somewhat old and tired, at times lacking in both innovation and dynamism. Extant theories of human resource management are all-too-often self-evident, and the empirical work is mostly predictable and unsurprising. If we could distill the lion's share of studies in HRM into one argument, it would be, quite simply, that employers should select, develop, train, and appraise the best people, treat them with respect and dignity, and pay them a fair wage, lest they respond with counter-productive work behaviors or organizational exit. Predictably, most studies in the field of HRM play on some variation of this argument, and so it is, therefore, hardly surprising that even the latest papers in the top human resources journals fail to elicit much excitement and debate. Indeed, an outsider to our field might reasonably conclude that we are nearing a saturation point.

Compare, for example, the state of HRM over the last 25 years to the concomitant developments in the cognitive neurosciences. Whilst for decades we have continued to argue, *ad nauseam*, that effectively implemented HR policies and practices are positively associated with both individual and organizational outcomes (see Arthur, 1994; Pfeffer, 1994; Huselid, 1995; MacDuffie, 1995; Becker and Gerhart, 1996; Ichniowski et al., 1997; Wood, 1999; Guthrie, 2001; Godard, 2004; Birdi et al., 2008; Guest, 2011, among others), cognitive neuroscientists and neuro-psychologists over this same time period have been busy making truly groundbreaking discoveries about how the brain works (for a good, accessible overview, see Presti, 2016). What's more, in spite of these breakthroughs, behavioral brain scientists still, to this day, understand just a fraction of the inner workings of its neural circuitry. Meanwhile, we HRM scholars often fall back on tautology to make the same, or very similar, arguments over and over again.

Fortunately, though, not all hope is lost for HRM. There are still frontiers to explore and unanswered questions, but in order to explore those frontiers and answer those questions, we must first learn to transcend our own disciplinary boundaries. To this end, Colarelli (2003) initiated what might be called a "biological turn" in management and organizations research, arguing that HRM should be aligned with evolutionary theory. A few years later, Wright and Diamond (2006) extended this biologization by pointing out that cardiovascular disease has important health implications, not only for employees, but also for organizations; White et al. (2006) showed that risk-taking behavior in organizations appears to be driven by high levels of testosterone; and Ilies et al. (2006) illustrated how a deeper understanding of behavioral genetics can throw useful light on management and employee behavior and decision-making. These studies were followed up a few years later by another key paper calling for an integration of human physiology with human behavior at work (Heaphy and Dutton, 2008). More recently, Becker and Cropanzano (2010) sought to explain organizational behavior from the point of view of the neurosciences. These initial exploratory linkages between neurobiology and human behavior at work were further strengthened by Lee et al. (2012) and, more recently, Nofal et al. (2018).

In short, there is an emerging wave of research suggesting that the future of HRM may well lie in a greater understanding of the natural sciences, with most of these scholars focusing on how biological and neuroscientific innovations can be fruitfully applied to the field of people management. This "biological turn" is a welcome development for our field, but it is, as yet, incomplete. One area that has not been thoroughly explored in much depth—that is, until this book—is the unique intersection between HRM and evolutionary psychology, also referred to as sociobiology (Wilson, 1975). There are two notable exceptions. Luxen and Van De Vijver (2006) explored the innovative link between facial attractiveness, sexual selection, and personnel selection using an evolutionary perspective, and Fruhen et al. (2015) found that the positive relationship between employee attractiveness and employee reward could be explained through the lenses of evolutionary psychology. The paucity of literature in this field, admittedly, may well be traced back to the widely negative views that have been expressed over evolutionary psychology (Gould, 1978), especially in the context of organization studies (Sewell, 2004; Nicholson, 2005). To be sure, there is no point in attempting to conceal the fact that evolutionary psychology has its explanatory problems, but, then again, so does every other theory across both the natural and social sciences. Let us not throw out the proverbial baby with the bathwater.

## WHAT IS EVOLUTIONARY PSYCHOLOGY?

Readers of this book are assumed to already possess some familiarity with human resource management (as both an academic field of study and a set of professional practices), but considerably less familiarity when it comes to the tenets of evolutionary psychology. So, let us start at the beginning. What do we mean by evolutionary psychology?

In order to understand what is meant by evolutionary psychology, we must first come to grips with the basic principles of evolutionary biology. The most pre-eminent evolutionary biologist of all time is, of course, Charles Darwin, the English naturalist whose fame derives largely from his scientific discoveries made during his *HMS Beagle* voyage to the Galápagos Islands, located off the coast of Ecuador in South America (for an excellent history of Darwin's journeys, see Browne, 1995). Darwin penned two of the most important scientific works of the last century and a half: *On the Origin of Species* (Darwin, [1859] 1998) and *The Descent of Man, and Selection in Relation to Sex* (Darwin, [1871] 2001). A thorough explanation of Darwin's theory of evolution and natural selection is well beyond the scope of this book—and, in any event, an extended summary can already be found elsewhere (Dawkins, 2006). But a brief overview of the field is probably of some utility at the outset of this book.

The underlying assumption of evolutionary biology is that organisms, or even genes within organisms (Dawkins, 1976), are programmed to survive in a competitive and at times dangerous environment. The survival instinct is built into the DNA of all living organisms, resulting in phenotypical traits that enable them to "project" their existence into the future. Contrary to popular belief, it is not always strength that facilitates survival. Indeed, the term "survival of the fittest" was coined not by Darwin, but rather by

Spencer (1884), the father of so-called "social Darwinism." Much more important than an organism's strength is, according to Darwin, its capacity for adaptation (Gould, 2002; Williams, 2008). In other words, genetic variations that are associated with an improved ability to adapt to a changing environment result in natural selection, whereby the most adaptable organisms survive and thrive and the least adaptable ones succumb to the realities of a harsh environment, only to wither and die eventually. The classic ethological example of this selection process is evident in Darwin's observations of the various finches found in the Galápagos islands. With an assiduous attention to detail, he noted that the same species of finch developed unique, idiosyncratic traits that appeared to be dependent upon the different sources of food across the various islands (see Grant and Grant, 2014).

Within this dynamic struggle to survive, the role of sexual selection and genetic heritability comes to be seen as the key driver of evolutionary processes. Obviously, all life is time-stamped with an inexorable expiration date; therefore, the only way to ensure long-term survival is through procreation and propagation. Within the animal kingdom, mate choice is the single most crucial mechanism for ensuring the survivability of an organism's offspring (Andersson and Simmons, 2006). In its inherent quest to propagate, the organism, using exquisitely developed perceptual machinery, must be capable of differentiation between potential mates that offer the highest (and indeed the lowest) chances of passing on superior heritable traits. In this way, over several millennia, a species ever-so-gradually evolves, in large part in response to the outcome of sperm competition to fertilize the female egg (Smith, 1984; Simmons, 2005).

One might well be questioning at this point what, on earth, sperm competition in the animal kingdom has to do with human resource management decision-making. In order to explain this as yet abstract linkage, we must now transition away from evolutionary biology and towards evolutionary psychology, the organizing framework of this book. Whereas *On the Origin of Species* (Darwin, [1859] 1998) outlines a theory of evolution in the animal kingdom, *The Descent of Man, and Selection in Relation to Sex* (Darwin, [1871] 2001), a lesser-known manuscript, was Darwin's subsequent attempt to draw together reasoned inferences from his evolutionary theory of animal behavior in order to explain human behavior. *Homo sapiens* are, after all, just one of the thousands of other Mammalian species on earth.

Evolutionary psychology, previously referred to as sociobiology (Wilson, 1975), is a growing field of study that aims to explain contemporary human values, beliefs, attitudes, and behaviors as a function of our experiences in the ancestral environment. It brings together psychology, ethology, ecology, biology, physiology, endocrinology, and neuroscience into one, overarching explanatory framework. In short, it seeks to explain *why* human beings today think, feel, and behave in the way that they do. Perhaps the best way to describe its explanatory power is with a series of practical examples. Consider the following questions and answers.

Question: why do modern humans suffer from insomnia and related sleep disorders? Answer: the evolutionary psychologist would argue that light sleepers in the ancestral environment held an evolutionary advantage over deep sleepers, the latter of whom were unlikely to awaken when a saber-toothed tiger entered their cave at night looking for a tasty snack. Question: why do women express a preference for taller men over shorter ones? Answer: the evolutionary psychologist would argue that tall men are, *ceteris paribus*, stronger than shorter men, implying that the latter would be less capable of protecting offspring from an attack by that same saber-toothed tiger or any other animal or indeed person. Question: why do men express a general preference for slim, younger women? Answer: the evolutionary psychologist would argue that weight and age are concomitantly associated with infertility and ill health, thus rendering older and overweight women sub-optimal from the point of view of childbearing and fecundity. Question: why do people engage in conspicuous consumption (Veblen, 1925)? Answer: the evolutionary psychologist would argue that ostentatious displays of wealth signal to potential mates a high social status, thus increasing the chances of conception and thus reproduction. Question: why are men with bigger penises generally seen by women as more desirable sexual partners than those with smaller penises? Answer: the evolutionary psychologist would argue that penis "lengthiness" signals virility and offers a reproductive advantage in copulation. An astute observer will have noticed a pattern emerging across all of these questions. At the very heart of all human (and animal) behavior is an innate, naturally selected drive to increase the probability of survival and reproduction.

Even a phenomenon like racial and ethnic prejudice, traditionally viewed through the lenses of the social psychology of inter-group relations (Tajfel, 1982; Abrams and Hogg, 1998), can be said, in the final analysis, to have evolutionary psychological bases. Whereas social psychologists can demonstrate that we have in-group preferences (Brewer, 1999) and mistrust of the out-group (Reik et al., 2006), they cannot readily explain *why* this is the case. Enter, evolutionary psychology. In the ancestral environment, individuals decided on whom to trust based on the extent to which the "other" resembled them. Kin were perceived to be most non-threatening and members of the same tribe or clan were seen as only moderately more threatening. However, foreigners, especially those of a different appearance or physical complexion, were viewed with immediate suspicion and mistrust. As a general rule, the greater the apparent genetic relatedness, the more apt we are to trust others (DeBruine, 2002), and vice versa. This "hard-wired" preference for the racial in-group may well explain the fact that a majority of people who claim to be racially egalitarian, in fact, still suffer from implicit or unconscious biases against members of racial groups other than their own (Greenwald et al., 1998), a theme that will be further explored in the final chapter of this book.

This point serves as an appropriate segue into a necessary discussion, or rather caveat, of what evolutionary psychology is *not*. Although an evolutionary psychological lens can *explain* human behavior, it does not, and should never be used to, *justify*, and especially *excuse*, the darker side of human behavior. This distinction is more than just splitting hairs. That human beings may well be predisposed toward prejudice does not imply concomitantly that prejudice is naturally inevitable and therefore defensible. As we will learn in the next chapter, we all possess both a biological self as well as a socialized self. At the intersection of these selves is the perennial and still vaguely understood battle between nature and nurture (Ridley, 2003). But neither the sociologist, nor the evolutionary psychologist, should seek to deny the role of genetics and the social environment, respectively, in terms of shaping human behavioral outcomes. In other words, evolutionary psychology, at least as it is presented in the context of this book, eschews genetic determinism and accepts that we are all capable of resisting, though perhaps not completely overcoming, our evolutionary impulses that were developed millennia ago in the ancestral environment.

In a similar vein, another important caveat worth noting at the start of this book is that evolutionary psychologists do not assume that all human beings are selfish egoists only concerned with individual survival and reproduction. Yes, compelling evidence exists that competition, hierarchy, and sexuality are undeniably central to human psychology and behavior, but then again, so are cooperation, egalitarianism, and sexual restraint. Indeed, the collectivist view of human behavior has been shown to be aligned with evolutionary theory, as demonstrated by Trivers' (1971) pioneering work on how "reciprocal altruism" can serve an adaptive function.

With these two caveats in mind, we are now ready to explore the question of how knowledge of evolutionary psychology can shine a new and exciting light on human resource management decision-making.

## THE APPLICATION OF EVOLUTIONARY PSYCHOLOGY TO HRM

This is mostly uncharted terrain. There is a huge amount of literature on evolutionary psychology and, separately, a huge amount on human resource management, but the unique intersection of these two fields is, with a few notable exceptions (Luxen and Van De Vijver, 2006; Fruhen et al., 2015, both described above), largely unmapped territory. This conspicuous lacuna provides an opportune opening for this book. The key research question at the heart of the study is, simply (or perhaps not so simply): are human resource management decisions ultimately rooted in evolved human preferences that are the result of adaptive selections that can be traced back to the dawn of humankind? Throughout this book, various evidences—mostly derived from experimental research designs—will be brought to bear on an evolutionary theory of HRM. In aggregate, they answer this research question in the affirmative.

Chapter 2 presents a theoretical model that sets the stage for the rest of the book. In it, a bio-psycho-social theory of workplace mobbing (also known as workplace bullying) is presented. Victims of mobbing, once expelled from the organization, often struggle to comprehend the depravity and savagery of the perpetrators' behaviors. Mobbing behavior is explained in this chapter as a natural biological response to a threatening work environment. Using evolutionary theory, the chapter describes human mobbing behavior as a function of the deeply embedded survival instinct within all of us.

Ethological evidence of mobbing behavior in the animal kingdom is presented in order to lay the foundations for the theory. It is then argued that an existential threat to one's employment, and thus livelihood, effectively "overrides" the more compassionate socialized self, allowing the egotistical biologic self to "govern" the actions of the individual and the collective behavior of the perpetrator(s). The theory explains how once "good" colleagues and friends can suddenly turn on the victim, unleashing a primal response aimed at the complete decimation and elimination of the threat from the workplace.

Chapter 3 presents what is very likely the first ever empirical study investigating the effect of variations in skin tone among Caucasian job applicants on their perceived employability in the U.S. labor market. It draws from the evolutionary psychology literature to explain employers' apparent aversion to lighter shades of white skin as a function of the perceived (ill) health and (un)attractiveness of the job applicant. Across three separate experiments, the chapter shows that lighter skinned Caucasians are viewed more negatively than those with normal skin tones and darker-than-average skin tones. Among women, it was found that darker skin tones are perceived as more attractive than normal skin tones, but this does not appear to affect employers' perceptions of job applicants' employability. This chapter makes an original empirical and theoretical contribution to the employee selection literature by drawing attention to a previously neglected form of employment discrimination based not on race, but rather on skin tone.

Chapter 4 explores the extent of employment discrimination against non-binary job applicants, i.e., those presenting as neither exclusively male, nor exclusively female. It uses social identity theory to explain why (mostly cisgendered) employers impose discrete male/female categorizations on job applicants. The results suggest that masculine-looking male applicants are rated significantly higher on perceived employability than feminized male applicants, feminine female applicants, and masculinized female applicants. A relative decrease in employability ratings between masculine men and feminized men was found in the experiment, but the same relative reduction was not found between feminine women and masculinized women. Again, this chapter contributes to the employee selection literature in its unique emphasis on understanding the effect of sexual dimorphism on labor market success (or failure).

Chapter 5 examines the previously unexplored question of whether job applicants with asymmetrical facial features are perceived as less employable in comparison to job applicants with symmetrical facial features. The study presents empirical evidence that hiring managers evince a preference for job applicants with symmetrical faces. It is argued that the tenets of evolutionary psychology may explain this finding. More specifically, evolutionary psychologists have posited that symmetrical facial features may signal attractiveness, health, and intelligence. It is, therefore, likely that hiring managers' preferences for job applicants with symmetrical features may well be rooted in our primitive sexual preferences evolved in the ancestral environment.

Chapter 6 concludes the book by examining the role of unconscious bias in human resource management decision-making. It focuses on how this bias shapes looks-centered recruitment and selection and performance management. The chapter argues that implicit biases exist "in the shadow" of consciousness and can impact HR managers' perceptions of potential and actual employees. The chapter draws on the neuro-psychology/neuroscience literature, highlighting how physical attributes, speech, and other mutable corporeal factors are important sources of implicit bias in HR decision-making. The book closes with a call for a more inter-disciplinary approach to studying HRM involving a team effort between the natural and the social sciences.

## CONTRIBUTION TO THE HRM LITERATURE

The value of all scientific research ultimately rests in its purported ability to advance knowledge above and beyond what we knew previously by, as it were, "standing on the shoulders of giants," to quote Sir Isaac Newton. Any study that fails to shine a new light on a previously underexplored phenomenon is worth only the paper it is printed on. Even studies that make a so-called incremental contribution to the literature by optimizing our previous understanding of a phenomenon are of limited value. To push the frontiers of science, what is needed, above all else, is the will to break free from disciplinary boundaries and to pursue truly inter-disciplinary solutions to innovative research questions. On this count, this book can be said, with some degree of confidence, to make an important contribution to the field of HRM decision-making, in much the same way that

Saad (2007, 2011) added value to our current understanding of the field of marketing. For those readers that manage to arrive at the end of this book, it is hoped that they will see HRM in a new and exciting light.

In the end, this book will have succeeded if it sparks more questions than it answers. It will be demonstrated that, although the threat of obsolescence (Dundon and Rafferty, 2018) is real, it is not inevitable. Indeed, the field of HRM may well be in its infancy. From evolutionary psychology to the cognitive neurosciences, a brave new world of knowledge awaits us as we step forward into the unknown world of what might be called "evolutionary HRM."

# 2. Understanding the evolutionary bases of workplace mobbing behavior: a bio-psycho-social model

The aim of this chapter is to articulate an evolutionary theoretical framework to explain workplace mobbing behavior. The extant literature on the pathology of workplace bullying is dominated by studies largely in applied psychology that focus on the antecedents of targeted psychological terrorism (Rayner, 1997; Hoel and Salin, 2003; Salin, 2003) as well as by research in public health that focuses on its epidemiological outcomes (Quine, 1999; Kivimäki et al., 2003; Nielsen and Einarsen, 2012). This large body of literature is classifiable across a number of dimensions, including, but not limited to: sectoral prevalence—where bullying is found to be more common in the public sector than the private sector (Hoel and Cooper, 2000; Salin, 2001); country of origin—where bullying is found to be more prevalent in northern European countries than in places where the termination of employment is less problematic (Leymann and Gustafsson, 1996; Einarsen et al., 2011); organizational culture—where bullying is found to be more prevalent in chaotic organizations with toxic leadership (Hodson et al., 2006; Lewis, 2006); personality types—where the perpetrators, victims, and bystanders have been found to exhibit unique dispositional traits (Pilch and Turska, 2015; Cohen, 2016); group identity—where members of socially disadvantaged or marginalized groups have been found to be disproportionately targeted by bullies (Fox and Stallworth, 2005; Willness et al., 2007); individual versus collective aggression—where the target is terrorized either by an individual bully or by a group mob (Leymann, 1996; Crawshaw, 2009); and the consequences for individuals versus organizations—where targeted employees face psychological, physiological, and career detriment (Mikkelsen and

Einarsen, 2002; Berthelsen et al., 2011) and organizations have been found to suffer from litigation, damaged morale, and staff turnover (Moayed et al., 2006; Hoel et al., 2011).

The lion's share of this literature is empirical (e.g., Einarsen et al., 2009), and many of the existing studies are descriptive, focusing mainly on the processes and critical incidents that were first identified in Leymann's (1996) classical treatment of the mobbing phenomenon. Although there have been some attempts at explaining mobbing behavior through established theoretical frameworks such as attribution theory (Rayner and Hoel, 1997), stress theory (Balducci et al., 2011), conflict theory (Zapf and Gross, 2001), stigma theory (Lutgen-Sandvik, 2008), and affective events theory (Branch et al., 2013), the workplace bullying literature is surprisingly light on theoretical development beyond this handful of studies. Whilst empirical data should always be welcome in any social analysis, collecting and analyzing them prior to sufficient theoretical scrutiny is akin to putting the proverbial cart before the horse.

There is any number of directions through which a theory of workplace bullying, or mobbing, could develop. For example, cognitive psychologists could build on the pioneering work of Brodsky (1976) to develop a theoretically informed typology of personality structures that are associated with both perpetrators and victims. Such a theory might allow for enhanced predictive modeling in recruitment and selection so as to avoid hiring employees or managers with latent psychopathic traits, or in the identification of employees susceptible to bullying so that they can be pre-emptively targeted for validated resilience training interventions. Social psychologists could expand on the established theories of prejudice (Allport, 1954) and social identity theory (Tajfel and Turner, 2004) to explain how and why the victim's identity is transmuted from the in-group to the out-group as a means by which to justify and rationalize the psychological violence inflicted upon him or her. Sociologists could draw from Berger and Luckmann (1966) to explain how and why, during the course of an internal investigation into a bullying claim, the employer might falsify evidence against the victim in order to cover up the abuse and protect the perpetrators. Any of these directions is potentially fruitful, but not the focus of this chapter.

One area of theoretical development that has not been explored previously—that is, until this book—is the investigation of workplace mobbing behavior through the lenses of evolutionary theory.

To be sure, such an approach rises to the occasion of recent calls for a strategic marriage between organization studies and biology (Heaphy and Dutton, 2008; Becker et al., 2011; Nofal et al., 2018). No one has previously asked whether the psychological violence that we inflict on one another in the workplace may be attributable to a built-in evolutionary neurological mechanism that enables survival and reproduction in a competitive and at times threatening environment. Whereas sociological treatments of workplace bullying and harassment may, at best, explain their proximate causes—e.g., the power differentials between the parties (Hodson et al., 2006; Lopez et al., 2009; McLaughlin et al., 2012)—an evolutionary treatment can be said to explain the ultimate cause: the primordial instinct to survive, which we share in common with every other organism on earth, past and present.

The survival instinct can be said to reside outwith the socialized self. It is ever present in complex human behavior (Hawkins, 1997), but also throughout the animal kingdom (Lorenz, 2002) and all the way down to the microbial and multicellular level (West et al., 2006). It is an adaptive mechanism that relies, when necessary, on violent aggression to eliminate existential threats (Buss and Shackelford, 1997). In humans, this evolved defense mechanism is in conflict with laws, institutions, and cultures that are designed to regulate destructive behaviors. Therefore, when an individual or groups unleash their primal instincts, they must either accept the structural (i.e., legal, institutional, or cultural) constraints and deal with the consequences of their actions or exert control over those structural constraints in order to reduce or eliminate punishments, similar to the ways in which criminals employ coercion over the justice system to evade prosecution (Kugler et al., 2005).

This chapter provides the first ever ethologically grounded investigation of workplace mobbing behavior. It presents an integrated bio-psycho-social theory that explains—but, as mentioned in the previous chapter, does not justify—the actions of a workplace mob. It takes as its starting point that human beings, like all of the other organisms on earth, are driven by biological impulses to survive and thrive (Dawkins, 2006). *Homo sapiens* are distinguishable from all other species on earth in that they possess a socialized self, that is to say, a socially constituted identity that sets out a system of morality that governs our interactions (Mead, 1967: 379–389). However, it is argued here that, under conditions of threat, human beings are apt to sacrifice their socialized selves, thus allowing their biological impulses to control their behaviors.

This is an important topic of investigation because of the profound and severe effects of mobbing on victims. The consequences are well documented in the empirical literature. Leymann (1990) estimated that, at the end of the 20th century, 10 to 15 percent of all suicides in Sweden were the result of perceived workplace mobbing behavior. Groeblinghoff and Becker (1996) point not only to the psychological and psychosomatic effects of mobbing, but also to the occupational and earnings detriment that many victims experience. Balducci et al. (2009) demonstrate that workplace mobbing is directly associated with increased paranoia and neuroses, along with post-traumatic stress disorder and suicidal ideation. Duffy and Sperry (2007) show that the negative effects of mobbing extend through the victim and into his or her family as well. Moreover, it is also very likely that the prevalence of workplace bullying, estimated in a recent meta-analysis to be, on average, 14.6 percent of employees (Nielsen et al., 2010), may be dramatically underestimated due to the confidentiality clauses in settlement agreements that victims often sign as they are constructively dismissed (Easteal and Ballard, 2017: 52).

In the next section of the chapter, some preliminary definitions are set out and the mobbing process described. This is followed by a review of ethological theories of mobbing in the animal kingdom. After that, an overview of the human survival instinct is proffered. An integrated bio-psycho-social theory of workplace mobbing is then presented, followed by a critical discussion in which a contribution to the literature is documented and suggestions for future research outlined. The chapter draws to a close with a brief conclusion and a summary of its main arguments.

## PRELIMINARY DEFINITIONS AND PROCESSES

There are subtle differences and similarities between workplace bullying and mobbing (see Zapf and Einarsen, 2005). The key distinction is that bullying is generally viewed as dyadic (Aquino and Lamertz, 2004)—with a single perpetrator and a single victim—whereas mobbing is always multivalent. Archetypical mobbing entails a group effort to expel an individual target from the workplace (Hogh et al., 2011). This chapter focuses exclusively on the group dynamics underlying the workplace mob and its impact on the victim. The focus on mobbing is justifiable on the basis of the fact that there is already a useful theory explaining dyadic bullying (cf. Aquino and Lamertz, 2004).

Crawshaw (2009: 264) ponders the definitional complexity of psychological aggression in the workplace by listing out some 33 related terms that essentially describe this phenomenon, including: *"abuse, abusiveness, aggression, bullying, bullying/mobbing, counterproductive workplace behavior, emotional abuse, emotional harassment, employee emotional abuse, generalized workplace abuse, harassment, hostile workplace behavior, maltreatment, mistreatment, mobbing, nonphysical aggression, nonsexual harassment, non-status-based harassment, psychological abuse, psychological aggression, psychological harassment, psychological terror, scapegoating, status-blind bullying, status-conscious bullying, unlawful bullying, vexatious behavior, workplace abuse, workplace aggression, workplace harassment, workplace hostility, workplace incivility, workplace psychological violence"* (italics in original). Arguably, the commonest definition of workplace mobbing is that provided by Leymann (1990, 1996), who specifically distinguishes workplace mobbing behavior from temporary workplace conflicts. In short, he defines mobbing as systematic psychological terrorism and violence, occurring at least once a week for over six months, inflicted by a group against an individual. One remarkable feature of this definition is that it describes mobbing as a form of violence, but the damage is primarily psychological, as opposed to overtly physical (Spector et al., 2007). From the point of view of the perpetrator, psychological violence is preferable to physical violence because it is highly damaging to the victim, yet leaves no visible scar as evidence of wrong-doing.

Drawing from Leymann (1990, 1996), Figure 2.1 visually depicts the temporal process by which mobbing behavior typically emerges, develops, and terminates, although this process is, in practice, always multi-causal and rarely linear (Zapf, 1999). Mobbing behavior

*Figure 2.1    The Basic Workplace Mobbing Process According to Leymann (1990, 1996)*

frequently originates with a "critical incident" that triggers the mob. This is usually a minor conflict, one that is based on inter-personal tensions that may have been simmering for quite some time. Following the critical incident is normally an attempt at informal resolution which, if unsuccessful, often results in the target filing a formal grievance against the perpetrators (Peterson and Lewin, 2000; Keashly and Nowell, 2003; Jenkins, 2011), thereby intensifying the resolve of the mob. This formalization gives rise to the involve-ment of the human resources manager, who has been previously described as "a wolf in sheep's clothing" (Lewis and Rayner, 2003). The ensuing workplace investigation (Merchant and Hoel, 2003) overwhelmingly tends to protect the most powerful actors, typically managers who have been involved in the bullying (Vandekerckhove and Commers, 2003; Tepper, 2007). Throughout these informal and formal processes, the instigators incite others to inflict increasing levels of psychological violence against the target by recruiting managers, co-workers, as well as subordinates to join in on the campaign of terror. Common tactics involve, among others: leveling false accusations (e.g., of bullying) against the target and initiating disciplinary procedures, excluding the target from staff meetings and ostracizing him or her from the workplace, spreading rumors, intimidating the target through aggressive body language, making veiled threats, pointing to fabricated "performance" problems, and so on (Lutgen-Sandvik et al., 2007; Einarsen et al., 2009; Robinson et al., 2013). The process ultimately culminates in the expulsion of the target from the workplace (Shallcross et al., 2008), ideally through voluntary resignation or, failing that, through dismissal (constructive or otherwise).

The key actors, both internal to the organization and external, are described in Table 2.1. As with the temporal process depicted in Figure 2.1, it is important to caveat Table 2.1 with a disclaimer that not all of these actors are present in every instance of workplace mob-bing. Obviously, within an organization, mobbing always involves a target and perpetrator(s), but there are often active and passive roles for other actors. The three potential managerial actors include line managers, senior management, and human resources professionals (Boddy, 2011; Woodrow and Guest, 2014; Fox and Cowan, 2015). Typically, their interests in the mobbing process align with protect-ing the reputation of the organization and, where they are also the perpetrators, protecting themselves. When a grievance has been

*Table 2.1   Key actors in the mobbing process*

| Internal Actors | External Actors |
| --- | --- |
| "The Target" | "The Medical Doctor" |
| "The Perpetrator(s)" | "Lawyers" (for both sides) |
| "Human Resources" | "The Employment Judge" |
| "Line Managers" | "Mediators and Conciliators" |
| "Senior Management" | "Trade Union Representatives" |
| "Occupational Health"* | "Family" |
| "The Grievance Committee Members" | "Friends" |
| "Active Mob Participants" | |
| "Passive Mob Participants" | |
| "Secret Supporters" | |

*Note:*   *   Occupational health can be an internal or an external actor in this process.

filed, members of the grievance committee are also important actors inasmuch as they have the power to "define the situation," regardless of the facts of the case (Goffman, 1959). Relatedly, occupational health professionals can potentially play a key role in protecting the target (Vartia et al., 2003), although the fact that they are paid by the organization implies that their interests ultimately align with management. The last set of internal actors in the mobbing process are the bystanders (Paull et al., 2012; Mulder et al., 2014, 2017), which can be divided into three categories. "Active" mob participants inflict direct psychological violence on the victim at the behest of the instigator(s); "passive" mob participants are cognizant of the mobbing behavior of others, but do nothing to intervene on behalf of the target; "secret supporters" are colleagues who offer some support to the victim, but always in secret, lest they themselves become targets of the mob.

In addition to these internal players are a set of external actors who also have an important part to play in the mobbing process. Medical professionals are almost always involved in supporting the target in light of the devastating physiological and psychological effects of the mob (Nolfe et al., 2007; Nielsen and Einarsen, 2012). A trade union can also be a potential source of support for the target (Hoel and Beale, 2006), although, in an era of union–management partnerships (Oxenbridge and Brown, 2004), many labor unions are quick to sacrifice an individual member to gain favor with the

employer. Occasionally, workplace mobbing behavior results in litigation (Martin and LaVan, 2010), thus involving, variously, media-
tors, conciliators, lawyers, and employment judges. The last major
external actors include the friends and family of the target, many of
whom suffer from mob "spillover" effects (Duffy and Sperry, 2007).

The processes and key actors discussed in this section have received
significant scholarly attention, and yet one might argue that the
phenomenon of workplace mobbing is, with a few exceptions (e.g.,
Rayner et al., 1999; Bowling and Beehr, 2006; Einarsen et al., 2011;
Hackney and Perrewé, 2018), under-theorized, as argued above.
Although several studies have sought to explain mobbing behavior
as a function of individual, organizational, and social factors (Zapf,
1999; Salin, 2003; see also chapters 8, 9, and 10 in Einarsen et al.,
2003), these can be thought of as proximate causes. No one—that
is, until this chapter—has attempted to theorize what might be the
ultimate cause of mobbing behavior. To get at the very roots of this
phenomenon, we now turn our attention to the animal kingdom.

## AN ETHOLOGICAL THEORY OF MOBBING

It may seem curious at first glance to explain a social phenomenon
from the perspective of animal behavior, but evolutionary psychologists have long argued that human interaction is inseparable from
that of their non-human counterparts (Daly and Wilson, 1999). To
illustrate this point, in a study of the metaphors that are used by the
victims of workplace mobbing, Tracy et al. (2006: 168) report that
targets described themselves as "defenseless prey" and their abusers
as "ruthless animals." These descriptors point in the direction of a
potential theoretical link between workplace mobbing and ethology.
The aim of this section is to lay the foundation for this link.

Lorenz (1931) pioneered the study of mobbing in the animal
kingdom. Drawing from Darwinian evolutionary theory, he argued
that mobbing is an instinctive social attack on an "eating enemy"
(Lorenz, 2002: 23). When a member of the group recognizes an
imminent threat to their survival or existence, the response is
immediate, collective, primal, frenzied, and relentless. The "alerting
others hypothesis" is frequently viewed by behavioral ecologists as
an adaptive evolutionary response to danger (Curio et al., 1978).
The response is thought to be just as natural and innate as any other

primitive function, such as sexual reproduction and the consumption of food and water—two behaviors that we share in common with most animal species. The majority of instances of animal mobbing are inter-species, where there is often a power imbalance between the rivals (see also Keashly, 1997). Typically, the less powerful species relies on collective force to overpower a more robust predator, whereas the opposite is true in most instances of workplace mobbing (Girardi et al., 2007).

The most common examples of animal mobbing in the literature involve birds. Pavey and Smyth (1998) document the mobbing of owls by 44 different species of forest birds, concluding that the behavior posed a high risk to the mobbers, but paid off by reducing the probability of predation. Drawing from anti-predatory theory, Griesser and Ekman (2005) examined the mobbing behaviors of Siberian jays on models of hawks and owls, concluding that mobbing is particularly ferocious in the presence of offspring and kin. This study is especially insightful inasmuch as it appears to mimic the principles of social identity theory, whereby the interests of the in-group are prioritized over and above those of the outgroup (Ashforth and Mael, 1989). Pettifor (1990) found that avian mobbing was driven by the need to expel predators from their foraging territories. Examples of non-avian mobbing behavior also abound. Graw and Manser (2007) document extensive antipredator mobbing on the part of meerkats. Gursky (2005) reports instances of primate mobbing behavior against serpent predators. There is even evidence that Australian fur seals, when threatened, will mob a great white shark (Kirkwood and Dickie, 2005).

The very fact that animals across a variety of species engage in mobbing suggests that this behavior may similarly be "embedded" into the human psyche as a survival mechanism. Violence and aggression in the animal kingdom are, by definition, instinctive, so it is likely that aggressive behaviors may also manifest pre-cognitively in human beings. Having said that, animal mobbing is still distinct from workplace mobbing on a number of fronts. Most obviously, whilst both animals and humans can be said to act on instinct, only the latter possesses a truly socialized self (Freud, 2015). Whereas traditional Watsonian behaviorism posits a simple stimulus–response model, social behaviorists recognize that the stimulus and response are always mediated by the human mind (Mead, 1967). Accordingly, there is no element of morality in animal mobbing, although the presence of ethics cannot be denied in instances of workplace mobbing. The second key distinction is, as noted above, that the "victim" in animal mobbing is usually a much larger, more powerful predator, whereas workplace mobs tend to target more vulnerable and emotionally unstable people (Glasø et al., 2007). Finally, whereas animal mobbing is usually a response to an immediate threat to life, the "danger" is perhaps less imminent in the case of workplace mobbing, as described in the next section.

## THE SURVIVAL INSTINCT IN HUMANS

Anthropological evidence points to widespread violence across cultures and history (Whitehead, 2004; Accomazzo, 2012). Evolutionary psychologists have argued that humans in the ancestral environment developed "sophisticated perceptual and inferential machinery" (Barrett, 2005: 200) to cope with potential threats. One of the first and most obvious threats to our ancestral foragers were other animals. When confronting a potential predator, early humans used exquisite perception and inference to anticipate the intentions of the animal and thus predict its behavior ("Am I food, or is it food?"). When a potential threat was identified, an automatic fear response (Buss, 1997) prepares the body for evasion. Where "flight" is not possible, they face a simple choice: "kill, or be killed." This fight-or-flight response can be said to be a universal human instinct that enabled survival in a competitive and hazardous environment (Jansen et al., 1995).

In addition to fearing animals, we have also grown accustomed to fearing each other. Duntley (2005: 245) even goes so far as to argue that "[o]ther humans are the predators we should fear the most." Interpersonal violence in the ancestral environment was widespread as a mechanism to ensure reproductive success, but, obviously, the criminal justice system in modern society restrains our homicidal impulses (Daly and Wilson, 1988). Thus, in a "kill, or be killed" situation, rather than commit actual murder and face justice, modern humans often inflict costs by assaulting a rival's status, or reputation, as is the case in many instances of workplace mobbing (Lutgen-Sandvik, 2008). Whilst the damage of a psychological assault may seem, at first glance, less catastrophic than murder, in many cases they achieve the same objective; workplace mobbing is, for example, strongly associated with suicidal ideation (Nielsen et al., 2015), and so offers the perpetrator a "back door" to pro-actively eliminate a human life without having to commit murder. Furthermore, one of the most frequent causes of homicidal ideation is loss of status (Duntley and Buss, 2011), implying that mobbing not only inflicts violence against the target, but can, in unusual circumstances, also result in counter-violence directed against the perpetrator (see Lankford, 2013).

In this light, it is easy to imagine how the workplace, as a unique social context, can elicit violence and aggressive behavior among employees (Neuman and Baron, 1998). It is, in many ways, a con-temporaneous microcosm of the ancestral environment, one that is similarly characterized by predator–prey adaptations (Barrett, 2005: 220). Fundamentally, employees crave physiological security and safety (Maslow, 1943), and they achieve these ends largely through gainful employment; moreover, although the sudden termination of employment does not necessarily imply destitution and starvation—thanks in great measure to the modern welfare state—it certainly implies a loss of status as a potential mate (Komarovsky, 2004), a reduction in both mental (Murphy and Athanasou, 1999) and physi-cal (Wadsworth et al., 1999) health, and a real threat to the viability of one's offspring (Christoffersen, 1994). From this perspective, when a perpetrator's livelihood is threatened, he (less often, she; see Einarsen and Skogstad, 1996) is liable to set aside his moral code and to fall back on his primal instincts to eliminate the threat, often through the help of a mob.

In short, the target is effectively decimated, either psychologically or physiologically, as the perpetrator mobilizes the collective. The fear response is immediately activated in both the target and the perpetrator, and to varying degrees across the mob participants as they are drawn into the conflict. In parallel with identified threats in the wild, the key to success in the conflict is to eliminate the rival, or at the very least to expel the target from the immediate territory (that is, the workplace); an objective that is most effectively and efficiently achieved through "coalitional violence" (Campbell, 2005). The key question here, of interest to both social psychologists and evolutionary psychologists, is whether the primal fear system takes precedence over our higher level cognitive and moral processes, as argued by Öhman and Mineka (2001). This question is explored in the following section.

# AN INTEGRATED BIO-PSYCHO-SOCIAL THEORY OF WORKPLACE MOBBING

The faint contours of an evolutionary theory of workplace mobbing have emerged slowly thus far. The purpose of this section is to solidify that theory. The overarching premise of the conceptual framework presented here is that all human beings possess a socialized self that, when threatened, is then sacrificed by a biological self driven by survival instincts. This biological self is activated when an individual feels threatened or vulnerable, at which point we become, in essence, more animal than human—hence the need to introduce this theory with an overview of ethological mobbing behavior. Indeed, whether human beings are capable of incalculable depravity is not in question (Zimbardo, 2007); what is up for debate, however, are the various explanations as to *why* seemingly good people commit unspeakable acts against each other. In the case of dyadic workplace bullying, the violence can readily be explained as a function of the perpetrator's individual psychopathic personality traits (Baughman et al., 2012), but this explanation is much less convincing in a collective mobbing situation, for obvious reasons. In what follows, a processual model of the development of a workplace mob, based largely on Leymann (1996), is elucidated in order to provide an alternative, evolutionary explanation.

*Stage 1: Pre-Critical Incident.* Prior to the critical incident that triggers the mob, the eventual target is not a target at all, but rather just a colleague and, oftentimes, a friend. All employees in the organization, including the eventual target, are members of the in-group and they interact with each other as individual socialized selves with a common identity and "background assumptions" (Timming, 2010). At this early stage, there are no interpersonal threats to individual fitness, and it is even possible that the eventual target is a friend of the eventual perpetrator(s), as is common in cases of childhood bullying (Mishna et al., 2008). In this early stage, the primacy of the socialized self ensures mutual respect, trust, and dignity in the workplace (Sayer, 2007).

*Stage 2: Critical Incident.* The critical incident, first identified by Leymann (1990, 1996), is the point of conception of the mob. At this stage, the mob does not yet exist except in the form of a potentiality. The eventual target and the eventual perpetrator find themselves in a state of "liminality" (Beech, 2011) between the socialized self and the biological self. Both parties know that *something* has happened, but they are not yet sure how to react. The triggering event most often involves some degree of wrong-doing on the part of the eventual perpetrator. For example, whistleblowing commonly triggers a mobbing response (Bjørkelo, 2013), where the eventual target witnesses illegal or unacceptable behavior. Ironically, low level bullying, or "robust management," on the part of the eventual perpetrator against the eventual target is also a common trigger, leading to victimization or retaliation (Skarlicki and Folger, 1997). This can be referred to as the "bullying paradox," where a complaint against genuine bullying is met with a tidal wave of reverse bullying, oftentimes in the form of false accusations of bullying behavior leveled against the target.

*Stage 3: The Grievance.* Depending on the degree of wrong-doing on the part of the perpetrator, conciliation may be possible prior to the target filing a grievance. At this stage, the perpetrator, and typically the employer as well, make attempts to informally resolve the conflict, but if the behavior of the perpetrator is particularly egregious, the seeds of discord have already been sown. The mere fact that the target witnessed the perpetrator's wrongful behavior is oftentimes enough to activate the latter's fear response. When a formal grievance has been filed by the target accusing the perpetrator of misconduct, the perpetrator's socialized self, in effect, shuts down as the biological self takes control. In terms of neural functioning, those areas of the perpetrator's brain responsible for empathy (e.g., the bilateral anterior insular cortex and the medial/anterior cingulate cortex, see Lamm et al., 2011) are over-ridden by the fear response, which is located in the amygdala (Davis, 1992), near the hippocampus. The perpetrator's job, livelihood, and thus biological fitness, are now perceived to be in jeopardy, depending on the outcome of the grievance investigation.

*Stage 4: The Investigation.* The perpetrator at this stage views the target's grievance as a threat to life. Both sides now generally understand that the only course of action is to "kill, or be killed," metaphorically speaking. Duntley (2005) argues that the key evolutionary strategy of defending against an attack is "turning members of a group against the person who may intend to kill you" (p. 237). The target is thus violently forced from the in-group to the out-group, resulting in a sudden and dramatic re-configuration of social identities (Marques and Paez, 1994). The workplace mob is activated as the fear response disperses across the organization. The attack against the target becomes, as with animals (Lorenz, 2002), frenzied and relentless, the key difference being that typically only psychological violence is inflicted. As colleagues are drawn into the mob, they similarly, driven by a self-preservation instinct, sacrifice their socialized selves in the name of survival. Alignment with the target, at least publicly, is impossible because to do so would automatically convert the bystander into a co-target for elimination from the organization. This biologization of the process peaks at this stage as the socialized selves recede into the background.

*Stage 5: The Expulsion.* The target of the mob is almost always expelled from the workplace, often joining the ranks of the long-term unemployed as a result of post-traumatic stress disorder and comorbid conditions (Mikkelsen and Einarsen, 2002). He or she is left psychologically broken and at the risk of accompanying somatization (Hansen et al., 2006). The fate of the perpetrator(s) is less certain. In the case of managerial (Vandekerckhove and Commers, 2003) or supervisory (Tepper, 2007) abuse, the organization almost always aligns itself with the mob inasmuch as their interests overlap. However, on occasion, managerial perpetrators are brought to justice through the investigatory process. Only when the mob has completed its mission of expelling the target from the workplace does the fear response subside, provided that there are no pending legal proceedings against any of the perpetrators (Martin and LaVan, 2010). The socialized self then re-emerges, although it will likely be forever cognizant of the primacy of the biological self.

Figure 2.2 illustrates the key components of this processual framework. This process follows the descent of modern humans into a Hobbesian state of nature in which our behavior is governed not by socially accepted norms of conduct, but rather by our evolved impulses, developed over millennia as an adaptive solution to what we perceive (rightly or wrongly) as an existential threat. Embedded into this process is a bio-psycho-social theory of human behavior, where the folkways and mores of the socialized self (Sumner, 1940) wither and die before the awesome power of evolutionary adaptations. If workplace mobbing can be said to be an intellectual battlefield between the sociologist and the evolutionary psychologist, it would seem that the latter has an edge in this instance. In a similar vein, to the extent that workplace mobbing is a struggle between good and evil, right and wrong, one might argue, again, that the latter has prevailed. None of this is meant to invalidate sociological

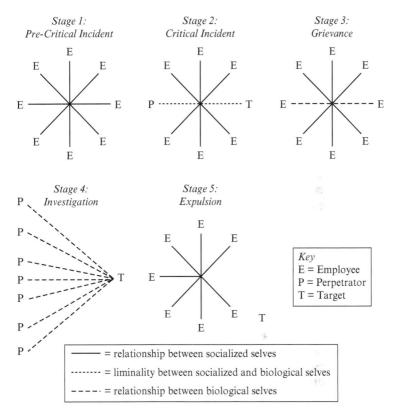

*Figure 2.2     A bio-psycho-social model of workplace mobbing*

explanations of identity and behavior, but rather to suggest, in this context at least, that the "bio" can override the "social" in explaining the "psycho" (pun intended).

## ULTIMATE VERSUS PROXIMATE CAUSES

In the immediate aftermath of a workplace mob, the target, once expelled from the organization, frequently struggles to understand exactly what happened to him or her, as exemplified by one of Tracy et al.'s (2006) participants: "I kept thinking, *why? Why* did that happen? *Why? Why* did it have to happen? Why was someone so deceitful . . . why?" (italics in original). The sudden transformation of their position, from close friend to bitter enemy, oftentimes leaves them shocked, bewildered, and struggling for an explanation. The extant literature on workplace mobbing offers up any number of individual (Zapf and Einarsen, 2003) and organizational (Hoel and Salin, 2003) antecedents of the phenomenon, each of which is an important, albeit incomplete, piece of the puzzle. At the individual level, bullying behavior has been explained by high self-esteem and threatened egotism on the part of the perpetrator (Baumeister et al., 1996) and by low self-esteem and psychological vulnerability on the part of the target (Matthiesen and Einarsen, 2001). At the organizational level, it has been argued that bullying behavior is a function of institutional, contextual, or environmental factors (Einarsen, 2000), including unequal relations of power and toxic leadership. These explanations are useful contributions to knowledge, but they still only shed light on the proximate causes of mobbing behavior.

Scott-Phillips et al. (2011) distinguish between proximate explanations and ultimate causes in the context of evolutionary behavioral theory. They argue that so-called proximate explanations illustrate *how* a phenomenon works, whereas the ultimate cause explains *why* it works. Thus, one could argue that a combination of sociological (e.g., unequal power relations, see Hodson et al., 2006), psychological (e.g., psychopathological leadership traits, see Hoel et al., 2010), and economic (e.g., the pervasive threat of job insecurity, see De Cuyper et al., 2009) factors, in concert, "cause" workplace mobbing, but it is only by peeling back these proximate explanations that one can arrive at the core of an onion. In this case, the ultimate cause of the mobbing behavior is hypothesized here to be our pre-cognitive self-preservation impulses, developed over millennia, which have been argued throughout this chapter to take precedence over our socialized selves in times of uncertainty and insecurity.

The fact that we observe mobbing both in the animal kingdom and in organizations could be just a coincidence, or it could say something about the enduring and ubiquitous nature of the "kill, or be killed" impulse common to all organisms, from microbes to higher-order animals and human beings—the latter of whom have been described by Nietzsche (2006: 176) as the "cruelest animal" of all. This is, of course, not to suggest that people are incapable of Lockean kindness and goodwill. On the contrary, the socialized self governs the lion's share of our quotidian interactions, even in the workplace. But when our survival is perceived to be at stake, we show ourselves to be wolves in sheep's clothing, figuratively speaking.

## ADVANCING FUTURE RESEARCH

The bio-psycho-social theory outlined in this chapter does not easily lend itself to empirical testing. This is, arguably, a critique that could be leveled against the whole of evolutionary psychology (Sewell, 2004). In a now classic essay, Gould (1978) accuses evolutionary psychology of being nothing more than "speculative storytelling." Although he recognizes that evolutionary behavioral stories are "plausible," he argues that they are often presented "without evidence or test, using consistency with natural selection as the sole criterion for useful speculation" (p. 531). To the extent that science is assumed to advance only through Popperian falsification (Ketelaar and Ellis, 2000), evolutionary psychology may rightly be viewed as a series of "just-so" stories. But the same could be true of evolutionary biology, where testable hypotheses are few and far between and the overall integrity of the framework is based on the principle of inference to the best explanation (Lipton, 2004).

The difficulties of carrying out value-adding empirical work in relation to this theory notwithstanding, it is worth having a discussion about how the evolutionary bases of workplace mobbing might be explored, if not tested, empirically. A peculiar feature of the theory—which distinguishes it from the lion's share of research on bullying at work—is its attempt to explain mobbing *behavior*, thus making the perpetrator(s) the focus, rather than the experience of the targets. It should not be surprising that most empirical research on mobbing involves data collection from targets or victims (Tracy et al., 2006; Lutgen-Sandvik, 2008; Shallcross et al., 2008; Efe and Ayaz, 2010). Perpetrators are, understandably, reluctant to talk openly about their exploits as a result of social desirability bias—although it may be possible to reduce this bias through anonymous online surveys (Joinson, 1999). Nevertheless, qualitative interviews or survey research with perpetrators might not yield enough fruit to put the theory to the test, as it were. Moreover, it is not entirely clear how future researchers might measure the biological self using traditional social science epistemologies.

Observational field studies are also largely off the table. Whereas

ethologists can readily observe mobbing behavior in the animal kingdom (Lorenz, 1931; Pettifor, 1990; Pavey and Smyth, 1998; Griesser
and Ekman, 2005; Gursky, 2005; Kirkwood and Dickie, 2005; Graw
and Manser, 2007), the same cannot be said of an organizational
anthropologist. At best, an ethnographer might be able to observe
the effects of mobbing on the victim—for example, that he or she has
been ostracized and excluded from meetings or is increasingly taking
sick leave—but that is quite separate from explaining the behavior
and mindset of the perpetrator(s), which is the unique focus of this
chapter.

In spite of the dwindling options for further empirical research
on this topic, not all hope is lost. The most promising direction
for future research is to use experimental designs that employ a
combination of social indicators (to measure the socialized self)
and bio-indicators (to measure the biological self). Obviously, no
ethical review board would allow even simulated bullying against
real human subjects, but it may be possible to create virtual mobbing
scenarios where the behavioral choices of participants are evaluated
using a battery of psychometric scales and instruments, including
the MMPI-2 (Matthiesen and Einarsen, 2001; Balducci et al., 2009),
the Negative Acts Questionnaire-Revised (Einarsen et al., 2009), the
Barrett Impulsiveness Scale (Patton et al., 1995), and the authoritarian personality (TAP) inventory (Adorno et al., 1950; Timming and
Johnstone, 2015), among others. In addition, participants in a simulated workplace bullying scenario could also be subject to a number
of biological, neuropsychological, and endocrinological assessments.
This might involve the monitoring of hormone production (e.g.,
testosterone, epinephrine, and cortisol) as well as brain imaging
studies of the fear response (in the amygdala and hypothalamus)
and impulse control (in the orbitofrontal cortex). Other bio-markers
that could also be measured include heartbeat, blood pressure, and
perspiration. In concert, all of these indicators should throw a light
on the biological underpinnings of workplace mobbing.

In the final analysis, it may well be impossible to "prove," or indeed
disprove, any evolutionary theory. Even evolutionary biologists
cannot offer incontrovertible evidence of the theory of evolution, in
spite of their efforts to argue otherwise (Coyne, 2010). But rejecting
evolutionary theory on that basis is essentially like throwing out
the baby with the bathwater. Acceptance of the plausibility of the
theory presented in this chapter requires a paradigm shift away

from Popperian falsificationism and towards inference to the best explanation (Harman, 1965). This approach is based on abductive logic wherein the scientific method is viewed as a puzzle in which data come together to form the simplest and most reasonable explanation of a phenomenon or process. Thus, multiple hypotheses are proposed and the best explanation emerges victorious, that is, until a better explanation is put forward. Therefore, perhaps the most important contribution of this chapter to future research is, in closing, an open invitation to other social and natural scientists to engage in a debate surrounding the validity of the bio-psych-social model presented here and, where possible, to offer up a better explanation.

## CONCLUSIONS

Victims of workplace mobbing are unlikely to find any consolation from this analysis. By the same token, although the perpetrators may now perhaps better understand *why* they did what they did, the explanation provided here is certainly not an excuse for their behavior. That mobbers have succumbed to their visceral instincts by sacrificing their socialized selves in the name of survival in no way justifies the mob itself, nor does it provide any good rationale. The chapter does, however, level a robust critique against those who argue that human beings are intrinsically good (Rousseau, 2013), or at least against those (primarily sociologists) who argue that human beings are not intrinsically bad (Jackson and Rees, 2007). In the centuries-old debate on human nature, this chapter adds further weight to the pessimistic view.

# 3. Skin tone as a cue to employability: sociology against evolutionary psychology

The preceding chapter introduced the idea of a debate of sorts between sociological and evolutionary psychological explanations of behavior. This chapter extends that debate through an empirical analysis, the first of its kind, on the effect of Caucasian job applicants' skin tone on perceived employability. There is, of course, a huge, primarily sociological, literature, developed over the last few decades, supporting the widely accepted claim among sociologists that the U.S. labor market, in particular, is blighted by structural racism (Bonilla-Silva, 1996), such that white job applicants, *ceteris paribus*, enjoy relatively greater access to employment opportunities than their non-white counterparts (Wilson, 1997; Massey and Denton, 2003), many of whom are subjected to explicit harassment (Mong and Roscigno, 2010) and implicit forms of prejudice and discrimination (Deitch et al., 2003). The consensus within this literature is that whiter skin is an asset and darker skin is a liability (Hunter, 2007). Even among non-white races, lighter skin has been found to be more advantageous in the labor market than darker skin (Arce et al., 1987; Hill, 2000; Espino and Franz, 2002; Hunter, 2002). As a result, in parts of the world, non-whites have subjected themselves to harsh skin bleaching to achieve a "fairer" complexion (Easton, 1998; Charles, 2003; Hall, 2006).

Whilst it seems clear that whiter skin is generally preferred to darker skin in cross-racial interactions and within non-white races (especially in the employment arena), we do not know whether, or to what extent, Caucasians job applicants with "fairer" complexions might enjoy superior employment outcomes vis-à-vis Caucasians with darker hues. Some contrary evidence has emerged in the field of evolutionary psychology suggesting that whites with *darker* skin tones could be perceived more positively than whites with lighter skin tones. Evolutionary psychologists view skin tone as an honest bio-logical signal of health amongst Caucasians. For example, Stephen et al. (2009a, 2009b) show that a darker, reddish skin tone signals highly oxygenated blood, which in turn leads to increased perceptions of good health (Armstrong and Welsman, 2001). It has also been found that, amongst Caucasians, darker skin colorations (Jones et al., 2004) and color homogeneity (Matts et al., 2007) are associated with perceived attractiveness, which can be an important proxy for employability (Morrow, 1990). In short, this chapter aims to discover whether a darker skin coloration among white job applicants is an asset or a liability, thus comparing and contrasting extant sociologi-cal and evolutionary psychological theories.

The key contribution of this research is to the muddy literatures on the effects of skin tone, especially on employment outcomes. Disparate voices within this multi-disciplinary body of work have emphasized the merits of both lighter and darker complexions. The data collected for this chapter, it will be shown, only partially corroborate extant research on the evolutionary psychology of skin tone: it does not appear that darker skin tones are associated with improved outcomes, but rather that lighter skin tones are associ-ated with reduced outcomes. Across three experiments, it will be demonstrated that, in general, lighter skinned Caucasians are viewed more negatively on perceived employability, perceived health, and attractiveness compared to their darker skinned counterparts. The results reported here lend some credibility to the view that employee selection decision-making may be driven, at least in part, by a set of "evolved preferences" (Luxen and Van De Vijver, 2006) that have developed over millennia based on our experiences in the ancestral environment.

In the next section, the relevant sociological and evolutionary psychological literatures are reviewed, setting out the key debate at the heart of this chapter. After that, the research methods of three separate empirical studies are described and the results reported and discussed in turn. These three sections are followed by a general discussion of the main findings and an outline of some directions for future research.

# THE SOCIOLOGY OF RACE AND THE MERITS OF LIGHTER SKIN

Sociologists have generated a huge body of research over the years investigating the effects of skin color on various life outcomes. Written largely from the perspectives of social identity theory (Calhoun, 1994; Hogg et al., 1995; Rockquemore et al., 2009) and critical race theory (Feagin et al., 2001; Golash-Boza, 2016; Delgado and Stefancic, 2017), this literature points to an overwhelming advantage for whites over non-whites, especially as pertains to labor market position. On most of the leading labor market indicators, Caucasians fare better than the majority of other races. For example, white people enjoy significantly higher wages than non-whites (Grodsky and Pager, 2001); they are less likely than non-whites to be terminated or made redundant in an economic downturn (Couch and Fairlie, 2010); they are more satisfied with their jobs than non-whites and also receive higher evaluations of job performance from managers (Greenhaus et al., 1990). The advantages of lighter skin also cut across gender, with most white women faring significantly better in the labor market than non-white women (Neal, 2004). Looking at the big picture, lighter colored skin, almost across the board, improves one's labor market position. This result was even reproduced in empirical studies of skin tone among black men, where it is found that lighter skinned African Americans receive higher wages than their darker skinned counterparts (Goldsmith et al., 2006). In short, it is widely agreed among sociologists that, "the lighter one's skin tone, the better one is likely to fare economically and socially" (Jones, 2000: 1498).

This generalized preference among managers for employees and job applicants with lighter hues over darker complexions has been replicated time and again and so does not require further corroboration. However, the unique impact of variations in lighter and darker skin tones on employment outcomes among Caucasian job applicants is a largely unexplored research question. This omission from the literature is directly addressed in this chapter, which goes beyond the largely sociological studies of race and ethnic relations and turns toward the literature on evolutionary psychology to explain how, and why, skin tone appears to impact the perceived employability of Caucasian job candidates.

# EVOLUTIONARY PSYCHOLOGY AND THE MERITS OF DARKER SKIN

Although it has weathered its fair share of criticisms in recent years (Sewell, 2004), evolutionary psychology is, as suggested in previous chapters, a powerful analytic framework that has been employed fruitfully to explain human behavior. As we have seen, evolutionary psychologists seek to explain human values, attitudes, preferences, and behaviors as a function of our latent, animalistic impulses to reproduce and survive in a precarious environment (Barkow et al., 1992; Buss, 1995, 2005). Evolutionary psychologists posit that we choose our sexual partners, friends, and associates based on signals, or visual cues, displayed by others suggesting health (Jones et al., 2001; Fink et al., 2006; Rhodes, 2006) and intelligence (Zebrowitz et al., 2002; Kanazawa and Kovar, 2004; Prokosch et al., 2005), two characteristics that are seen as essential to our long-term individual and collective survival. It is postulated in this chapter, and throughout this book, that employee selection and sexual selection may well draw from similar neural mechanisms inasmuch as managers and sexual partners value, respectively, employees and mates that present as healthy, intelligent, and attractive.

Skin coloration is one of many physiological traits that evolutionary psychologists have argued is an important cue to health, survivability, and good genes, at least among Caucasians. Researchers have found that whites with darker, tanned skin tones are generally perceived as more attractive than whites with lighter skin colorations (Fink et al., 2001; Smith et al., 2007; Chung et al., 2010), although it has also been suggested that these preferences may vary across cultures (Swami et al., 2008). The reason underlying our preference for darker shades of white skin when it comes to mate choice is that a dark reddish skin coloration indicates high levels of hemoglobin (Matts et al., 2007) as well as elevated blood oxygenation levels (Stephen et al., 2009a, 2009b), signaling cardiovascular and circulatory health, both of which implicitly communicate reproductive quality. Primatologists have similarly noted that a reddish facial coloration among rhesus monkeys is an important cue to mate quality (Waitt et al., 2003).

Among evolutionary psychologists, there is a plethora of evidence suggesting that, within Caucasians, melanin colorations in the face signal health (Jones et al., 2016; Pezdirc et al., 2018) and, relatedly, attractiveness (Stephen et al., 2012; Lefevre and Perrett, 2015). Alternatively stated, a whiter skin coloration is potentially associated with reduced perceptions of health and attractiveness. If true, this finding stands in contrast to the sociological literatures pointing to a set of advantages associated with lighter skin, although it is recognized that skin tone and race, whilst certainly related, are still qualitatively different constructs. Crucially, for purposes of the research presented in this chapter, it is not known how, or whether, variations in skin color might affect the perceived employability of Caucasian job applicants. It is on this key question that this chapter makes an important empirical contribution to the HRM literature.

According to evolutionary psychological theory, we can expect the following patterns to emerge in our data. These patterns are expressed here as hypotheses, three of which are proposed in this chapter:

*H1:*   *White job applicants with darker skin tones are perceived as more employable than white job applicants with lighter skin tones.*

*H2:*   *Whites with darker skin tones are perceived as healthier than whites with lighter skin tones.*

*H3:*   *Whites with darker skin tones are perceived as more attractive than whites with lighter skin tones.*

We will also explore whether gender may interact with skin tone in relation to perceptions of employability, health, and attractiveness, although this dimension is not presented as a specific hypothesis, but rather explored through a series of moderations.

Three separate experiments that speak to these hypotheses are now described in turn.

## EXPERIMENT 1

### Research Methods

### Stimuli
A good experiment first requires the creation of good stimuli. To this end, eight photographs, four male and four female Caucasians of a

similar age and physical build, were selected from a publicly available database of facial images. Each photograph was taken at a 0° angle, with a neutral expression, and under constant lighting. The eight original (hereafter, "baseline") images were standardized for inter-pupillary distance to promote comparability. These images were then modified using a popular digital face manipulation tool that can alter the cosmetic features of the face. Two stimuli groups were created using this digital tool. In the first group, all eight baseline images were given a lighter-than-normal ("whitened") skin complexion. In the second group, all eight baseline images were given a darker-than-normal ("reddened") skin complexion. Thus, the experiment employed 24 test photographs: eight baselines with natural colored white skin, eight stimuli with whitened skin, and eight stimuli with reddened skin. Another eight diversionary photos were included in the experiment so that participants would not assume *a priori* that the study is "about" skin tone.

**Data collection**
In order to approximate real-world employment conditions for the experiment, only respondents that were, at the time, employed as practicing managers were targeted. Participants first responded to some demographic questions (years of management experience, gender, age, race, and employment sector). They were then immediately presented with these instructions:

> *Imagine that you are recruiting an employee for the most typical role in your organization. We will now show you some photographs of potential job applicants for this role. Assuming that all applicants are roughly equally qualified, how would you rate the following job candidates on a scale of 1 to 7, where 1 means it is NOT AT ALL LIKELY and 7 means it is EXTREMELY LIKELY that you would hire this person?*

The 32 test faces (eight baseline faces, eight whitened faces, eight reddened faces, and eight diversionary faces) were then presented to the participants in randomized order, one at a time. The order of presentation of the faces was determined using a random number table to prevent the respondents from identifying a pattern.

Following Oppenheimer et al. (2009), an instructional manipulation check was built into the survey instrument as a quality control mechanism to screen for careless participants. Two items in the questionnaire were randomly placed to evaluate whether respondents were paying attention: a simple arithmetic problem ("What is 8 + 3?") and another item that listed out 11 hobbies, but asked participants to select the two beginning with the letter "r" ("reading" and "rugby").

The instrument was administered using a popular online crowd-sourcing platform whose samples have been found to be just as reliable as, and even more diverse than, traditional ones (Buhrmester et al., 2011). In total, 232 participants initially completed the survey, all of whom were located in the United States. After deleting cases that failed the manipulation check, the final sample size is N=219 managers. Of these, 49.8 percent of respondents are female; the average age is 36.87 years (s.d.=10.07); the participants reported an average of 6.03 years of management experience (s.d.=4.90); 78.1 percent of the respondents are white, 10.5 are black, 4.1 are east Asian, 2.3 are south Asian, 0.5 are American Indian, and 4.6 are mixed race; 63.9 percent are employed in the private sector (services), 8.2 in the private sector (manufacturing), 21.5 in the public sector, and 6.4 in the non-profit sector.

**Analysis**
Composite variables were created for both the male and female test faces, separately. The composites were then re-scaled to the original 7-point Likert. A mixed design analysis of variance (ANOVA) was used to test H1. The statistical analyses decompose the employability ratings by skin tone (*light* v. *baseline* v. *dark*), job applicant gender (*male* v. *female*), and participant gender (*male manager* v. *female manager*). Thus, a 3×2×2 model was estimated, with participant gender entered as a between-subjects variable.

**Results**

Table 3.1 reports the main effects of the repeated measures. There was a main effect of skin tone ($F_{(2,434)}=159.66$, $p<0.001$, $\eta_p^2=0.424$) on employability, with respondents rating the whitened skin lowest (M=4.13, SE=0.07), alongside higher scores for the reddened skin (M=4.61, SE=0.06) and the baseline, or natural color, skin (M=4.64, SE=0.06). The main effects for sex of face (*male* v. *female job applicants*) and sex of respondent (*male* v. *female managers*) were not found to be statistically significant.

Separate Bonferroni-corrected pairwise comparisons were generated to further explore the main effect of skin tone on employability.

*Table 3.1  Main effects of 3×2×2 mixed design ANOVA for study 1 on employability*

| | Effect type | Mean rating (SE) | Mean rating difference | F | p | $\eta_p^2$ |
|---|---|---|---|---|---|---|
| Skin Tone (Whitened; Baseline; Reddened) | Within-subjects | Whitened: 4.13 (0.07) Baseline: 4.64 (0.06) Reddened: 4.61 (0.06) | Whitened-Baseline=−0.51 Whitened-Reddened=−0.48 | 159.66 | <0.001 | 0.424 |
| Job Applicant Gender (male; female) | Within-subjects | Male: 4.44 (0.06) Female: 4.48 (0.07) | −0.04 | 0.684 | 0.409 | 0.003 |
| Manager Gender (male; female) | Between-subjects | Male: 4.55 (0.08) Female: 4.36 (0.08) | −0.07 | 2.724 | 0.100 | 0.012 |

*Table 3.2     Results of the 3×2 interaction between skin tone and sex*
*of job applicant for study 1 on employability*

| Job Applicant Gender | Skin Tone | Mean (SE) |
|---|---|---|
| Male | Whitened | 3.84 (0.08) |
| | Baseline | 4.79 (0.07) |
| | Reddened | 4.68 (0.07) |
| Female | Whitened | 4.42 (0.07) |
| | Baseline | 4.50 (0.07) |
| | Reddened | 4.54 (0.07) |

*Note:*    $F = 128.56$, $p < 0.001$, $\eta_p^2 = 0.372$

It was found that the whitened job applicants were rated significantly lower than the baseline skin job applicants ($F(1,217) = 209.77$, $p < 0.001$, $\eta_p^2 = 0.492$) and the reddened skin job applicants ($F(1,217) = 176.25$, $p < 0.001$, $\eta_p^2 = 0.448$). However, the difference between the baseline skin job applicants and the reddened skin job applicants was found to be statistically insignificant, suggesting that any additional reddening of the face beyond its normal hues does not appear to improve perceived employability.

There was a significant 3×2 interaction effect between skin tone and sex of face ($F(2, 434) = 128.56$, $p < 0.001$, $\eta_p^2 = 0.372$). The results of this interaction are reported in Table 3.2 and depicted graphically in Figure 3.1. It would appear from Figure 3.1 that whitened skin only moderately dampens the employability of the female job applicants, but it seems to strongly reduce the employability of the male job applicants. In order to examine this interaction effect more closely, six separate paired sample t-tests were carried out. To correct for potential familywise error across these tests, a more conservative p-value of 0.01 was used ($0.05/6 = 0.01$).

First looking at the male job applicants, it was found that the whitened faces were rated significantly lower on employability than the baseline faces ($t(218) = -18.40$, $p < 0.001$) as well as significantly lower than the reddened faces ($t(218) = -16.74$, $p < 0.001$). It was also found that the baseline faces were rated higher on employability than the reddened faces ($t(218) = 3.33$, $p = 0.001$). Looking now at the female applicants, there was only one statistically significant finding. The whitened faces were rated significantly lower on employability than the reddened faces ($t(218) = -2.72$, $p = 0.007$). There were no dif-

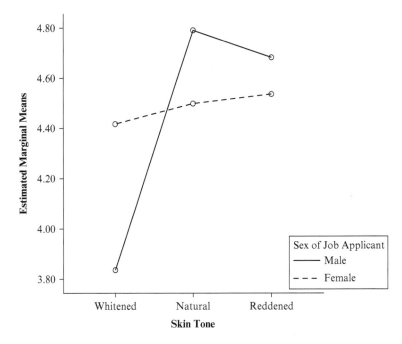

*Figure 3.1    Graphical representation of the 3×2 interaction between skin tone and sex of job applicant for study 1 on employability*

ferences between the whitened faces and the baseline faces, nor were there any differences between the baseline faces and the reddened faces.

## Discussion

The results of Experiment 1 confirm H1, but only partially. At the main effects level, a whitened skin color among Caucasian job applicants is associated with reduced employability, but redder colorations beyond the normal hues failed to increase employability. It would seem that, for white applicants at least, whiter skin tones are a liability in the labor market, but darker skin tones are perhaps not an asset. When job applicant gender is interacted with skin tone, the effect is somewhat more muted for women than for men. Among female Caucasians, whitened skin corresponded to lower employability ratings or, alternatively stated, reddened skin corresponded to higher employability ratings. Among male Caucasians, the whitened skin was not only rated lower than the baseline skin and reddened skin, but it was also found that the reddened skin was rated lower on employability than the baseline skin. Thus, for men, it would appear that natural skin optimizes employment chances.

This generalized preference on the part of employers for Caucasian job applicants presenting with baseline skin over lighter skin challenges extant sociological literature pointing to the benefits of fairer skin over dark skin (Arce et al. 1987; Greenhaus et al., 1990; Hill, 2000; Grodsky and Pager, 2001; Espino and Franz, 2002; Hunter, 2002, 2007; Neal, 2004; Goldsmith et al., 2006; Couch and Fairlie, 2010). Whilst these purported benefits may manifest in cross-racial studies and among non-whites, they are not evident among Caucasians. This is an important finding in its own right, but it is insufficient in and of itself. Although Experiment 1 has established that fairer skinned Caucasians are perceived by managers as less employable than their baseline and darker skinned counterparts, there is no explanation of *why* this might be the case. To explore the "why" question, we now turn to Experiments 2 and 3.

## EXPERIMENT 2

### Research Methods

Experiment 2 replicates Experiment 1, except instead of asking managers to rate the photographs on perceived employability, a non-managerial sample of participants is asked to rate them on perceived health. This shift in focus allows the study to speak to H2. The survey instrument used in Experiment 2 presents the same faces in the same randomized order, but this time, respondents are asked to rate each photo on a scale of 1–7, where 1 means the person depicted is "NOT AT ALL HEALTHY" and 7 means the person depicted is "EXTREMELY HEALTHY." The same demographic questions were also asked, although the two items on management experience and employment sector were removed, given that this sample is non-managerial. Additionally, those respondents who completed the instrument for Experiment 1 were not allowed to completed the instrument for Experiment 2. The same instructional manipulation checks were also built into the instrument. In total, 248 participants, sourced from the same crowdsourcing platform, completed the survey. After removing 23 cases that failed the attention checks, the final sample is N=225. Whilst the proportion of females in Experiment 1's managerial sample was 49.8 percent, in this study, 61.8 percent are female. The average age is 38.54 years (s.d.=12.74). Moreover, 76.9 percent of participants are white, 8.9 percent black, 7.1 percent east Asian, 1.3 percent south Asian, 0.9 percent American Indian, and 4.9 percent were mixed race.

**Results**

Table 3.3 reports the main effects of the repeated measures. As with Experiment 1, there was a main effect of skin tone (F(2,446)=299.15, $p<0.001$, $\eta_p^2=0.573$), with the respondents rating the whitened skin lowest (M=3.76, SE=0.07) on perceived health, alongside higher scores for the baseline skin (M=4.79, SE=0.05) and reddened skin (M=4.79, SE=0.06). Also consistent with Experiment 1, the main effects for sex of face (*male* v. *female faces*) and sex of respondent (*male* v. *female participants*) were not statistically significant.

Separate Bonferroni-corrected pairwise comparisons were generated to further explore the main effect of skin tone on perceived health. The whitened faces were rated significantly lower on perceived health than the baseline faces (F(1,223)=366.15, $p<0.001$, $\eta_p^2=0.621$) and the reddened skin faces (F(1,223)=365.13, $p<0.001$, $\eta_p^2=0.621$). Because there was no difference in perceived health between the baseline skin and the reddened skin faces (both means=4.79), no further pairwise test was indicated. Thus, consistent with what was found in Experiment 1, there is no added benefit to perceived health by reddening a face beyond its normal hues.

Also consistent with Experiment 1, there was a significant 3×2 interaction between skin tone and sex of face (F(2,446)=104.25, $p<0.001$, $\eta_p^2=0.319$). The results of this interaction are reported in Table 3.4 and depicted graphically in Figure 3.2. Once again, it appears that the negative effect of whitened skin on perceived health is more muted for women than for men. In order to explore this interaction further, six separate paired sample t-tests were carried out, again using a more conservative p-value cut-off of 0.01 to mitigate against potential familywise error.

First looking at the male stimuli, the whitened faces were rated

*Table 3.3 Main effects of 3×2×2 mixed designed ANOVA for study 2 on perceived health*

| | Effect type | Mean rating (SE) | Mean rating difference | F | p | $\eta_p^2$ |
|---|---|---|---|---|---|---|
| Skin Tone (Whitened; Baseline; Reddened) | Within-subjects | Whitened: 3.76 (0.07) Baseline: 4.79 (0.05) Reddened: 4.79 (0.06) | Whitened-Baseline=−1.03 Whitened-Reddened=−1.03 | 299.15 | <0.001 | 0.573 |
| Sex of Face (male; female) | Within-subjects | Male: 4.47 (0.05) Female: 4.43 (0.06) | 0.04 | 0.695 | 0.405 | 0.003 |
| Sex of Respondent (male; female) | Between-subjects | Male: 4.51 (0.08) Female: 4.39 (0.07) | 0.12 | 1.169 | 0.281 | 0.005 |

*Table 3.4*   *Results of the 3×2 interaction between skin tone and sex of face for study 2 on perceived health*

| Gender of Face | Skin Tone | Mean (SE) |
| --- | --- | --- |
| Male | Whitened | 3.49 (0.07) |
| | Baseline | 5.00 (0.06) |
| | Reddened | 4.92 (0.06) |
| Female | Whitened | 4.04 (0.08) |
| | Baseline | 4.58 (0.06) |
| | Reddened | 4.68 (0.07) |

*Note:*   $F = 104.25$, $p < 0.001$, $\eta_p^2 = 0.319$

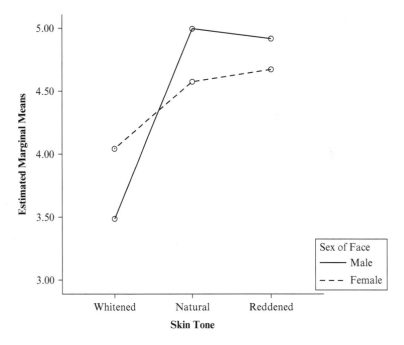

*Figure 3.2*   *Graphical representation of the 3×2 interaction between skin tone and sex of face for study 2 on perceived health*

*Table 3.5    Results of the 3×2 interaction between skin tone and sex of participant for study 2 on perceived health*

| Participant Gender | Skin Tone | Mean (SE) |
|---|---|---|
| Male | Whitened | 3.95 (0.11) |
|  | Baseline | 4.78 (0.08) |
|  | Reddened | 4.79 (0.10) |
| Female | Whitened | 3.58 (0.08) |
|  | Baseline | 4.79 (0.06) |
|  | Reddened | 4.80 (0.07) |

*Note:*   $F = 10.09$, $p < 0.001$, $\eta_p^2 = 0.043$

significantly lower on perceived health than the baseline skin faces ($t(224) = -21.58$, $p < 0.001$) and the reddened faces ($t(224) = -21.23$, $p < 0.001$). However, there was no difference in perceived health between the baseline skin faces and the reddened faces. Looking now at the female stimuli, the whitened faces were rated significantly lower on perceived health than the baseline faces ($t(224) = -9.63$, $p < 0.001$) and the reddened faces ($t(224) = -10.79$, $p < 0.001$). As with the male faces, there was no difference in perceived health ratings between the baseline skin faces and the reddened faces. Thus, for both men and women, a whitened face is perceived as less healthy, but a darker red face beyond a normal hue is not perceived as healthier.

Unlike in Experiment 1, however, there was a significant 3×2 interaction, this time between skin tone and sex of respondent ($F(2,223) = 10.09$, $p < 0.001$, $\eta_p^2 = 0.043$). The results of this interaction are reported in Table 3.5 and depicted graphically in Figure 3.3. It is apparent from Figure 3.3 that there is no significant difference between men's and women's ratings of the baseline skin faces and the reddened faces, but it seems that women rated the whitened faces lower on perceived health than men rated them. This difference was confirmed in a follow up independent samples t-test ($t(223) = 2.72$, $p = 0.007$).

**Discussion**

The data from this second experiment only partially confirm H2. Although it cannot be concluded that a reddened skin coloration beyond the normal hue is associated with increased perceptions of

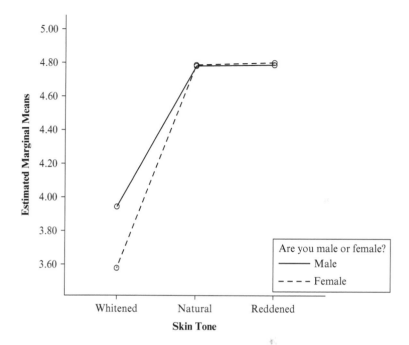

*Figure 3.3*    *Graphical representation of the 3×2 interaction between skin tone and sex of participant for study 2 on perceived health*

health, it can be concluded that a lack of coloration, manifested as a whitened skin tone, significantly reduces how healthy one appears to others. The results of Experiment 2, in the final analysis, suggest no difference on perceived health between the baseline and reddened faces, but the whitened faces are perceived as significantly less healthy than both the baseline and reddened faces. This finding is replicated for both male and female test faces. A key difference with Experiment 1, however, is that Experiment 2 revealed a between-subjects effect, such that women raters viewed the whitened faces as significantly more unhealthy than male raters.

These findings make a novel contribution to the extant literature on the evolutionary psychology of skin tone. Specifically, they suggest that, among Caucasians, a darker skin color may perhaps not be a cue to highly oxygenated blood and, by proxy, to improved circulatory and cardiovascular health (Armstrong and Welsman,

2001; Matts et al., 2007; Stephen et al., 2009a, 2009b; Jones et al., 2016; Pezdirc et al., 2018), but rather, the absence of a darker skin coloration (or the presence of a lighter skin tone) may be a cue to a low level of blood oxygenation and hemoglobin. Variations in skin tone, then, have more to do with perceived unhealthiness than with healthiness. Indeed, the fact that the lighter skin test faces were rated significantly lower on perceived health may potentially explain why they were also rated lower on employability. It would make sense to assume that employers are generally motivated to hire healthy workers, and this assumption is supported in the HRM literature (Novit, 1981; Cooper and Cartwright, 1994; Calderwood et al., 2016). Just as healthy mates may be perceived as more fecund, healthy employees may equally be perceived as more productive.

## EXPERIMENT 3

### Research Methods

Experiment 3 replicates Experiment 2, except instead of asking respondents to rate the photographs on perceived health, this time they are asked to rate them on attractiveness. The same photos, in the same randomized order, are presented to the participants, but now they are asked to rate them on a scale of 1–7, where 1 means that the person depicted is "NOT AT ALL ATTRACTIVE" and 7 means the person depicted is "EXTREMELY ATTRACTIVE." The same instructional manipulation checks were used, along with the same variables, plus the addition of one extra item that asked if respondents are attracted to members of the opposite sex. Respondents who participated in Experiments 1 and 2 were further disqualified from also participating in Experiment 3. The same online platform was used to crowdsource the data. In total, 249 participants initially completed the survey. A total of 29 cases were deleted as a result of the instructional manipulation checks and a further 21 cases were excluded to focus only on heterosexual attitudes, leading to a final sample size of $N=199$. The average age is 37.53 years (s.d.$=10.57$) and some 58.3 percent of the sample is female. Moreover, 76.9 percent of respondents are white, 8.5 percent black, 5.5 percent east Asian, 2.5 percent south Asian, and 6.5 percent are mixed race.

**Results**

Table 3.6 reports the main effects of the repeated measures. Consistent with Experiments 1 and 2, there was, again, a main effect of skin tone ($F(2,394)=97.15$, $p<0.001$, $\eta_p^2=0.330$), with the respondents rating the whitened skin lowest ($M=3.31$, $SE=0.07$) on attractiveness, followed by higher scores for the baseline skin ($M=3.80$, $SE=0.07$) and the reddened skin ($M=3.82$, $SE=0.07$). Unlike Studies 1 and 2, though, there was also a main effect for sex of face ($F(1,197)=84.63$, $p<0.001$, $\eta_p^2=0.301$), with respondents rating the female faces higher ($M=3.94$, $SE=0.07$) than the male faces ($M=3.35$, $SE=0.07$) overall. Sex of respondent was not statistically significant as a between-subjects variable.

Bonferroni-corrected pairwise comparisons found that, compared to the whitened skin, the baseline composites were rated significantly higher on attractiveness ($F(1,197)=112.15$, $p<0.001$, $\eta_p^2=0.363$). The reddened skin was also rated significantly higher on attractiveness compared to the whitened skin ($F(1,197)=124.96$, $p<0.001$, $\eta_p^2=0.388$). The female composites were also rated significantly higher on attractiveness compared to the male composites ($F(1,197)=84.63$, $p<0.001$, $\eta_p^2=0.301$).

Consistent with Experiments 1 and 2, there was a significant $3\times2$ interaction between skin tone and sex of face ($F(2,394)=47.93$, $p<0.001$, $\eta_p^2=0.196$). The results of this interaction are reported in Table 3.7 and depicted graphically in Figure 3.4. Notably, the male ratings are, across the board, all lower than the female ratings, and it appears, again, that the negative effect of whitened skin on attractiveness is more muted for women than it is for men. To explore this interaction effect further, six separate paired sample t-tests were carried out, again with a more conservative p-value cut-off of 0.01 to mitigate against potential familywise error.

First looking at the male stimuli, the whitened faces were rated significantly lower on attractiveness than both the baseline faces ($t(198)=-12.29$, $p<0.001$) and the reddened faces ($t(198)=-12.00$, $p<0.001$). There was no significant difference in ratings between the baseline faces and the reddened faces ($t(198)=2.07$, $p=0.04$), however, it is worth noting that this finding would have been significant had it not been for the adjustment to correct for familywise error. Looking at the female stimuli, the whitened faces were rated statistically significantly lower on attractiveness than the baseline faces

*Table 3.6  Main effects of 3×2×2 mixed designed ANOVA for study 3 on attractiveness*

| | Effect type | Mean rating (SE) | Mean rating difference | F | p | $\eta_p^2$ |
|---|---|---|---|---|---|---|
| Skin Tone (Whitened; Baseline; Reddened) | Within-subjects | Whitened: 3.31 (0.07) Baseline: 3.80 (0.07) Reddened: 3.82 (0.07) | Whitened-Baseline=−0.49 Whitened-Reddened=−0.51 | 97.15 | <0.001 | 0.330 |
| Sex of Face (male; female) | Within-subjects | Male: 3.35 (0.07) Female: 3.94 (0.07) | −0.59 | 84.63 | <0.001 | 0.301 |
| Sex of Respondent (male; female) | Between-subjects | Male: 3.64 (0.10) Female: 3.66 (0.08) | −0.02 | 0.03 | 0.860 | 0.000 |

*Table 3.7*  *Results of the 3×2 interaction between skin tone and sex of participant for study 3 on attractiveness*

| Participant Gender | Skin Tone | Mean (SE) |
|---|---|---|
| Male | Whitened | 2.83 (0.07) |
| | Baseline | 3.66 (0.08) |
| | Reddened | 3.58 (0.08) |
| Female | Whitened | 3.80 (0.08) |
| | Baseline | 3.95 (0.08) |
| | Reddened | 4.07 (0.08) |

*Note:*  F=47.93, p<0.001, $\eta_p^2$=0.196

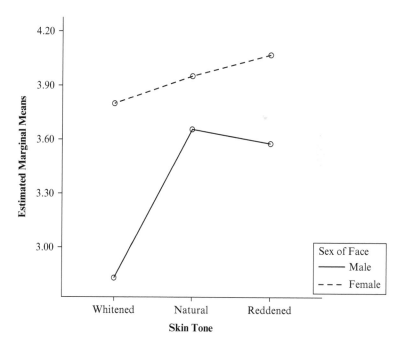

*Figure 3.4*  *Graphical representation of the 3×2 interaction between skin tone and sex of face for study 3 on attractiveness*

*Table 3.8    Results of the 3×2 interaction between skin tone and sex of participant for study 3 on attractiveness*

| Participant Gender | Skin Tone | Mean (SE) |
| --- | --- | --- |
| Male | Whitened | 3.38 (0.10) |
|  | Baseline | 3.76 (0.11) |
|  | Reddened | 3.77 (0.10) |
| Female | Whitened | 3.25 (0.09) |
|  | Baseline | 3.85 (0.09) |
|  | Reddened | 3.88 (0.09) |

*Note:*   $F=5.54$, $p=0.004$, $\eta_p^2=0.027$

($t(198)=-3.33$, $p=0.001$) as well as the reddened faces ($t(224)=-5.16$, $p<0.001$). It was also found that the reddened faces were rated significantly higher on attractiveness than the baseline skin faces ($t(198)=-2.72$, $p=0.007$). Notably, this is the only finding across the three experiments reported in this chapter showing a significant difference between the baseline skin and the reddened skin.

Unlike in Experiment 1, but like Experiment 2, there was a significant 3×2 interaction between skin tone and sex of respondent ($F(2,394)=5.54$, $p=0.004$, $\eta_p^2=0.027$). The results of this interaction are reported in Table 3.8 and depicted graphically in Figure 3.5. It is apparent from Figure 3.5 that women seem to give more extreme (high and low) ratings than men across the skin tones, and that both women and men are antagonistic toward whitened faces in relation to attractiveness. This interaction is decomposed further using six paired sample t-tests, once again using a p-value cut-off of 0.01 to correct for potential familywise error. First looking only at the male participants ($N=83$) and their ratings of the female faces, it was found that the whitened faces were rated lower on attractiveness than the baseline faces ($t(82)=-5.04$, $p<0.001$) as well as the reddened faces ($t(82)=-5.06$, $p<0.001$), but there was no significant difference in ratings between the baseline composites and the reddened composites. Now looking at the female participants' ($N=116$) ratings of the male faces, the same result was found, i.e., the whitened faces were rated lower on attractiveness than the baseline faces ($t(115)=-10.57$, $p<0.001$) and the reddened faces ($t(115)=-11.59$, $p<0.001$), but no significant difference in ratings was found between the baseline faces and the reddened faces.

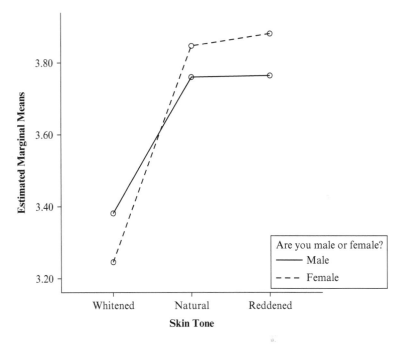

*Figure 3.5    Graphical representation of the 3×2 interaction between skin tone and sex of participant for study 3 on attractiveness*

## Discussion

Again, H3 is only partially confirmed by the data. At the main effects level, the same pattern as evidenced in Experiments 1 and 2 emerged, that is, attractiveness ratings are lower for the whitened skin compared to the baseline and reddened skin, but there is no extra benefit of reddened skin vis-à-vis the baseline skin. This finding is reproduced for the male faces, however, for the female faces, a darker red skin coloration is rated higher on attractiveness than the baseline skin tone. In other words, for women, H3 is fully confirmed by the data, but for men it is only partially confirmed. Thus, women with darker-than-normal hues are perceived as more attractive than those displaying natural skin tones, but the results of Experiments 1 and 2 suggest that these positive perceptions do not appear to spill over into concomitant increases in perceived health and employability.

These results generally corroborate extant research in evolutionary psychology linking perceived health to attractiveness (Jones et al., 2001; Rhodes et al., 2007; Re et al., 2011). That is to say that beauty may well be a function of sexual selection. There seems to be a remarkable consistency between perceptions of attractiveness and perceptions of health, with a distaste toward Caucasians with lighter, paler skin tones. The only notable difference is that skin tones that are darker-than-normal for women are seen by men as more attractive, but not necessarily as healthier. Similarly, there also seems to be an internal consistency between perceptions of attractiveness and employability, as confirmed in previous research (Morrow, 1990; Hosoda et al., 2003; Tews et al., 2009), with the only caveat being that women with darker-than-normal skin are perceived as more attractive, but not as more employable. Overall, it would be fair to surmise that perceptions of attractiveness, health, and employability appear to be intimately intertwined, with evidence of a general distaste for Caucasian subjects with lighter skin tones, a finding that challenges sociological studies that view lighter skin coloration as an asset, not a liability (Greenhaus et al., 1990; Grodsky and Pager, 2001; Neal, 2004; Couch and Fairlie, 2010).

## THE PALE PENALTY?

Lighter skin, at least among Caucasians, is widely associated with unattractiveness, ill health, and reduced employability. Darker, albeit natural, skin tones are generally preferred, with the one exception being that a darker-than-normal skin coloration among only women is perceived as more attractive. These findings have been discussed separately above. The purpose of this section is to outline how the aggregation of these studies makes an important contribution to the employee selection literature, to draw out some practical implications for job applicants and employers, and to recognize the limitations of the research reported in this chapter and set forth some directions for future research.

### Contribution to the Employee Selection Literature

Employment researchers often seek to explain organizational decisions by drawing from established theories that are subsequently transposed from the traditional social sciences (e.g., economics, sociology, psychology, and political science) to selection decision-making. Whilst there can be no broad generalizations about which social science is most "useful" as an explanatory framework, for the very specific research question examined in this chapter, one might well conclude that evolutionary psychology adds the most value. Sociologists have produced some truly excellent research on inter-race relations and the blight of structural racism (Bonilla-Silva, 1996; Wilson, 1997; Massey and Denton, 2003), and although they have conducted some fine within-race studies among non-white subjects (Arce et al., 1987; Hill, 2000; Espino and Franz, 2002; Hunter, 2002; Goldsmith et al., 2006), they have been conspicuously quiet on how variations of skin tone can affect outcomes among Caucasians. In contrast, evolutionary psychologists have made great strides in trying to understand this question. Their approach, at face value, is at least plausible. The argument that a darker, reddish skin coloration is preferable to lighter tones (Stephen et al., 2009a, 2009b, 2012; Re et al., 2011) is broadly confirmed here, although, as noted above, a more accurate conclusion is that lighter-than-average skin tones are widely rejected, whereas darker-than-average skin is virtually indistinguishable from normal skin tones (with the exception of perceptions of female attractiveness). All of this seems to suggest that, in regard to employee selection decision-making, we should not be dissuaded by extant critiques of evolutionary psychology (Sewell, 2004), and instead should try to accept, in light of the present study and others (Luxen and Van De Vijver, 2006), that the field of HRM could well benefit from thinking about personnel selection decision-making in much the same way that evolutionary psychologists think about sexual selection. Perhaps both employees and potential mates suffer from what might be called a "pale penalty."

**Practical Implications**

The research reported in this chapter has clear implications for both organizations and individuals. In respect to the former, employers ought to take notice of these results and recognize that, in addition to taking steps to obviate racial discrimination, they should also take steps to prevent what might be called skin tone discrimination. This might be uncharted territory for most organizations in that Caucasians are not perceived as a group that is subjected to disadvantage in the workplace. But the results reported here suggest that a certain sub-set of Caucasians can perhaps fall victim to an unconscious, or automatic, bias in employment decision-making (Devine, 1989). Employers ought to be especially aware of the possibility that lighter skinned Caucasian job applicants may well present as such in the light of an underlying health condition with visible dermatological symptoms. For example, it is widely recognized that sickle cell disease and thalassemia result in an iron deficiency that can lighten one's skin. Perhaps not coincidentally, and in support of the evolutionary psychological arguments made here, these diseases are associated with reduced blood oxygenation levels (e.g., see Rees et al., 2010).

The practical implications for job seekers and employees primarily fall within the remit of impression management (Goffman, 1963; DuBrin, 2011). Although there seems to be no employment benefit associated with darker-than-normal, or reddened skin, there is nonetheless an attractiveness premium for women. More crucially, however, for both male and female Caucasians presenting with a lighter-than-normal skin coloration, the results of the present study suggest that taking in some sun, or alternatively applying cosmetics, may neutralize any disadvantages one might face in a job interview. Obviously, this recommendation should only be pursued with proper medical advice, especially in the case of persons with an underlying health condition.

## Limitations and Directions for Future Research

No research, however well designed, is without its limitations, and the purpose of this section is to recognize the shortcomings of the experiments reported in this chapter and to make some recommendations for future research aimed at tackling them.

First, the experimental study design employed here should be complemented with field studies. It has been argued that "in the debate over alternative research strategies and settings, the problems of the laboratory are exaggerated, whereas many of the problems of field research are de-emphasized or completely ignored" (Dipboye, 1990: 25). Notwithstanding this defense of experimental designs, it would still be useful to explore the effect of variations in skin tone in organizational settings owing to the artificial conditions in experiments. This future research might similarly involve surveys, but could also entail qualitative interviews with both managers and job applicants surrounding these issues.

Second, though the use of three separate samples adds to the robustness of the findings, it also poses a methodological limitation. Specifically, by examining employability, perceived health, and attractiveness separately, it was not possible to analyze how these three outcomes interact. An experimental design, based on a single sample of managers responding to all three outcomes, would address this limitation. Methodologically, this could be achieved by using a multivariate analysis of variance (MANOVA) design in future research.

Third, as with most studies in face perception, the stimuli were created through digital manipulations. The advantage of digital manipulation is that the test images are standardized, aside from the factor of interest (in this case, skin tone variations), whereas between-subjects stimuli can introduce a number of visual confounds. That said, it may be useful to employ a set of between-subjects stimuli inasmuch as such manipulations might appear more "natural." This would involve, for example, photographing individuals after they have been deprived of, or subjected to, sunlight. The problem remains, though, how one might standardize the stimuli.

Fourth, this research has focused exclusively on variations in melanin coloration among Caucasians. Melanin is the pigment in Caucasian skin that gives it color and results in tanning in response to sun exposure (Slominski et al., 2004). However, recent evidence suggests that carotenoid coloration, which derives from the consumption of fruit and vegetables, may also be relevant to perceived employability. For example, Lefevre and Perrett (2015) recently found that "skin yellowness" also contributes positively to the perceived attractiveness of Caucasians and similarly enhances perceived health. Thus, future research should seek to replicate these three experiments, but using carotenoid-based, as opposed to melanin, stimuli.

Finally, at a conceptual level, it would seem that further theorization is needed on the exact nature of the relationship between skin tone and race. This chapter reports the results of a within-race investigation, but it addresses variations in skin color in much the same way that a between-race study might. Obviously, skin tone and race operate very differently, but perhaps there is less of a distinction than might be warranted. In any event, the idea that, among Caucasians, skin color can also lead to employment discrimination is a novel finding that could add value to the extant literatures on race and ethnic relations as well.

# 4. Gender fluidity at work: is sexual dimorphism an advantage in the labor market?

Social identity scholars have traditionally argued that the cognitive processes of categorization, both of inanimate objects and typologies of people, are fundamental to the human experience (Tajfel, 1981; Turner et al., 1987; Sherif, 2015; Hogg, 2016). They argue, under the umbrella of social identity theory, that we tend to make sense of the social world (Schutz, 1967), and ourselves (Swann Jr. et al., 2012), in relation to group memberships and by "compartmentalizing" other people into socially defined and constructed categories. Arguably, the commonest categorization in all of human history is that of "men" and "women," situated under the broad rubric of gender, and yet, even today, these sex roles are not fully understood as a result of the complicated interplay of biological, psychological, and social factors (Lorber, 1994). Evolutionary psychologists have shown that we have a built-in preference for faces that are sexually dimorphic, that is, sex typical (Barber, 1995; Perrett et al., 1998; Rhodes, 2006) in evaluations of attractiveness. Thus, men prefer "feminine-looking females" as mates, and women prefer "masculine-looking men" as mates.

But it has been argued more recently by sociologists that gender can also be seen as a non-binary social construct (Diamond and Butterworth, 2008; Ashcraft and Muhr, 2018) characterized by "fluidity" (Linstead and Brewis, 2004) and "multiplicity" (Linstead and Pullen, 2006). Thus, rather than thinking about gender identity in overly-simplistic, either/or terms, it is also possible to think of it as a continuum on which one can present a non-binary self or image that is neither male nor female, but rather somewhere in between. According to evolutionary psychologists (for an exception, see Little and Hancock, 2002), such individuals do not conform to the biological, sex typical norms of attractiveness (Cunningham et al.

1990; Jones et al., 1995), but no one has previously asked whether the non-binary might also suffer from discrimination in the labor market.

The idea of gender fluidity has received some limited scholarly attention, for example, by anthropologists studying the *hijra* ("third sex") in India (Nanda, 1999; Reddy, 2010) as well as by psychologists investigating androgyny in the wider gender schemata (Bem, 1981; Hoffman and Borders, 2001). Additionally, there is a sizable body of research on transgender identities (Gagné et al., 1997; Rubin, 2003), but the lion's share of this literature focuses on transitions from one gender to the other, rather than dwelling at any length on the implications of the continuum in between the two sex poles. The aim of this chapter is to examine whether gender fluid job applicants might suffer discrimination at work.

Following on from the research methods used in the previous chapter, an experimental approach is used to again simulate a job interview. This chapter shows that the evolutionary psychology of sexual dimorphism appears to explain discrimination against non-binary job applicants. The results presented here are important because they draw attention to a previously under-investigated source of implicit bias in the workplace. Specifically, this chapter suggests that "cisgendered" male and female managers (cisgendered can be defined as men who self-identify as men and women who self-identify as women), as a result of evolved mating preferences in favor of sexual dimorphism, may be discriminating against gender atypical job applicants and employees.

In the next section, the relevant literatures on social identity theory are reviewed and a series of informed research questions are developed. After that, the research methods by which the data were collected and analyzed are described. The results are then presented. The chapter draws to a close with a succinct recapitulation and discussion of the key findings reported here, an explanation of its contributions to the literature, an outline of its limitations, and some suggestions for future research.

## SOCIAL IDENTITY THEORY

Social identity theory (SIT), as conceptualized collectively by the contributors in Tajfel (2010), is, in many ways, a sociological manifestation of the basic principles of evolutionary psychology. The foundations of SIT stem back to a series of experiments looking at the categorization of physical (non-human) phenomena. Tajfel and Wilkes (1963) investigated participants' subjective evaluations of the lengths of eight separate lines, finding that, when broad classifications are superimposed upon the series (e.g., the four longer lines labeled "A" and the four shorter lines labeled "B"), the participants responded by exaggerating the extent of the differences by *overestimating* the length of the longer lines and *underestimating* the length of the shorter lines. This experiment was preceded a few years earlier by another classic categorization study that looked at a similar overestimation and underestimation of the magnitude of objects that have value to us (e.g., coins) vis-à-vis objects that have no value to us (e.g., metal discs), respectively (Tajfel, 1957). Taken together, these experiments point to a generalized tendency on the part of human beings to differentiate between categories through the processes of exaggeration and polarization.

These studies of inanimate phenomena were followed up over the last several decades by a number of investigations looking at how exaggeration and polarization also apply to inter-group human relations and organizations (Ashforth and Mael, 1989). For example, with a focus on political differentiations, Graham et al. (2012) found that liberals and conservatives in the U.S. significantly exaggerated the magnitude of moral differences across the two political parties. Ryan (1996) found that perceived cross-racial differences between black and white participants were significantly larger than actual differences. Crucially for purposes of this chapter, Hall and Carter (1999) found that individuals were widely inaccurate in describing gender stereotypes attributed to the opposite sex. Such are the differences between men and women that the two sexes are perceived by some scholars to be inexorable, natural, reified, and essentialized biological categorizations (Bohan, 1993). Others, however, argue that they are socially constructed, and therefore malleable, categories (Brickell, 2006).

In short, SIT provides an interesting conceptual fodder for contemporary thinking about gender fluidity at work. It assumes that individuals have a propensity to place each other into categories (male and female), and that, in order for us to more sharply distinguish between these social categorizations, we accentuate, perhaps even to the point of distortion, differences between men and women.

Such a view is wholly consistent with the evolutionary psychological literature on sexual dimorphism, which points to a general preference for masculine-looking men and feminine-looking women (Thornhill and Gangestad, 2006). However, as will be articulated in the next section, there is an increasing view, especially among sociologists, that gender is much more multifaceted than traditionally thought.

## A NON-BINARY APPROACH TO GENDER IDENTITY

Critical gender scholars have sought to "loosen ... [the] binary grip" (Ashcraft and Muhr, 2018: 206) of the traditional, male versus female, biologically- and anatomically-based sex roles. An emerging body of literature has recently pointed to the possibility that gender identity is a fluid concept, with a sizeable "gray area" in between masculinity and femininity. Butler's (1990, 1993) work on theorizing gender initially proposed the idea of thinking about "men" and "women," not as discrete and oppositional biologically determined sexes or social categorizations, but rather as a more nuanced, and essentially post-structuralist, part of the human condition (Prasad, 2012). Although perhaps an over-simplification of Butler's *oeuvre*, she argues that gender is not what one *is* biologically, but rather a performance that one *does* socially (West and Zimmerman, 1987; Fenstermaker and West, 2002), suggesting that all individuals have some choice, or agency, over their gender. Following in this same vein, queer theorists (e.g., Brewis et al., 1997; Parker, 2002) have similarly challenged what they call the hetero-normativity of the gender binary, pointing to the multiple ways in which sexuality can manifest and questioning the extent to which it is a stigma (Orne, 2013).

From the perspective of these feminist literatures, the problem with binary, sexually dimorphic gender categorizations is not just the fact that gender differences are exaggerated and polarized, but rather the fact that they also reproduce and reinforce hierarchies. Acker (1990), for example, demonstrated how that which is female, or feminine, tends to be devalued vis-à-vis that which is male, or masculine. Similarly, Dougherty and Hode (2016) point to the oppressive nature of the gender dichotomy, arguing that men are privileged at the expense of women. To the extent that women have value to men, that value is highly sexualized in a world of binary genders (Szymanski et al., 2011). Relatedly, yet another symptom of the gender dichotomy is that it creates, according to critics, oppressive standards of beauty for men and women, punishing those who fail to conform to the aesthetic ideal (Ruggs et al., 2015). The few studies that have investigated gender non-conformists (e.g., those who identify as neither men, nor women) highlight that such ambiguity is often met with revulsion, microaggressions (Nadal et al., 2016), and even physical violence on the part of cisgendered people (Wyss, 2004). As a result, those who present as non-binary are known to face a significant risk of victimization in daily life (Richards et al., 2016).

In short, whilst SIT and its adherents provide a theoretical rationale for the bifurcation of gender roles—primarily in the name of "cognitive simplification" (Oakes, 1996), a number of mostly feminist and queer scholars have concomitantly sought to re-frame this dualism by recognizing the continuity of non-biological sex identification across the gender spectrum. Though breaking free from this traditional gender dualism is possible—as evidenced by the increasing numbers of especially non-binary youths (Harrison et al., 2012)—the evidence also seems to suggest that gender non-conformists frequently face widespread discrimination in all walks of life, not only in sexual selection (Mao et al., 2018). The mistreatment of non-binary persons is arguably linked to the fact that gender fluid individuals fail to meet the rigid societal standards of cross-gender, sexually dimorphic attractiveness, and, therefore, incur the wrath of the gender typical majority (Doan, 2010).

## GENDER FLUIDITY IN THE WORKPLACE

Although studies have looked at employment discrimination against transgender people (Gagné et al., 1997; Davis, 2009), no previous research has evaluated in any depth the disadvantages specifically facing the non-binary community and its position within the labor market. We know, based on the extant evolutionary psychology literature, that gender non-conformists struggle to gain acceptance in a society that prizes sexually dimorphic features (cf. Mao et al., 2018), and we know that this struggle results in frequent victimization of the non-binary (Richards et al., 2016), but we still do not know how this victimization might impact on one's employment success (or failure). In a similar vein, there is also an extensive literature on gender discrimination in the workplace, much of which points to the myriad of obstacles that women confront in the labor market (see Hultin and Szulkin, 1999; Davison and Burke, 2000; Blau and Kahn, 2003; Arulampalam et al., 2007), but we still do not know much about the specific plight of non-binary people in the workplace. Finally, even in the event that the results of the experiment reported in this chapter produce some compelling evidence of employment discrimination against the non-binary, we still do not know precisely where, on the gender continuum, job applicants suffer the most, and whether cisgendered male and female hiring managers might have different attitudes toward, and therefore treatments of, non-binary job applicants.

Because of the general lack of previous literature on the impact of gender fluidity on one's labor market success or failure, this chapter poses a series of more exploratory research questions, rather than spelling out specific hypotheses *a priori*. The research questions include: (1) Are cisgendered job applicants rated higher on employability than non-binary job applicants? (2a) Is greater feminization of male job applicants associated with reduced employability? In a similar vein, (2b) is greater masculinization of female job applicants associated with reduced employability? Finally, (3) do cisgendered male and female hiring managers discriminate against non-binary job applicants differently?

## RESEARCH METHODS

In light of these research questions, it was decided once again to design and administer a survey to another sample of managers in order to assess potential discrimination against non-binary job applicants. However, two problems with this design immediately became apparent. First, it is likely that some of the participants would be unfamiliar with the meaning of "non-binary" when asked about it. Second, probing the participants about whether, or the extent to which, they discriminate against job applicants may result in a social desirability effect, such that few, if any, would admit to such discrimination. In order to overcome these problems, a visual methodology, whereby a set of photographs of non-binary job applicants are presented to the manager-respondents, was used in conjunction with indirect questioning to obviate social desirability bias (Fisher, 1993).

**Photographic Stimuli**

Two photographs (one male and one female, both Caucasians) were employed as the gender typical images and were taken from Rhodes et al. (2000). Black and white photographs were used to prevent the possibility of skin tone, or coloration (see previous chapter), emerging as potential confounds in the employability evaluations (Jones et al., 2004). These two faces, one "masculine male" and one "feminine female," represent the average of 24 male and 24 female faces whose photographs were morphed together through the use of face processing software. These gender typical photos were taken at a 0° angle, under constant room lighting, and with neutral facial expressions. They can be said to represent the average masculine male and the average feminine female and can be found in the first column of Figure 4.1.

Immediately to the right of these gender typical faces are four increasingly "feminized" men (first row) and four increasingly "masculinized" women (second row). Rhodes et al. (2000) created these "gender fluid" faces using the same face-morphing software. From left to right in Figure 4.1, each image represents an incrementally feminized/masculinized version of the gender typical photograph,

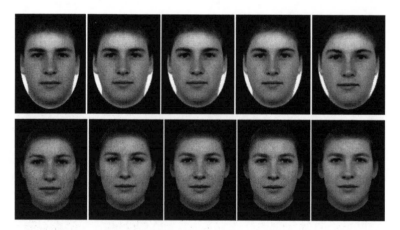

*Notes:* From top left to right: Gender Typical Male, GQ25% Male, GQ50% Male, GQ75% Male and GQ100% Male. From bottom left to right: Gender Typical Female, GQ25% Female, GQ50% Female, GQ75% Female and GQ100% Female.

*Figure 4.1    Baseline and stimulus images used in the experiment*

from GQ25% to GQ50%, GQ75%, and GQ100%, the latter of which is, in effect, a non-binary photograph where the subject is neither male, nor female.

In sum, the participants viewed these 10 photographs in the survey: one gender typical male and its four incrementally feminized versions and one gender typical female and its four masculinized versions. It should be noted that these photos have already been validated in Rhodes et al. (2000), therefore, we can be confident that they represent distinct levels of gender fluidity.

**Data Collection**

In order to bolster the external validity of the findings, and consistent with the sampling method in the previous chapter, only respondents currently employed as managers were targeted for inclusion in the sample. Qualtrics Panels (hereafter QP) were employed in order to source a sample consisting only of practicing managers. In other words, excluded from this sample are all participants not currently employed in a management position. QP draws from a national database of respondents located in the United States and applies strict quality control procedures, for example, screening and attentional checks, in order to ensure that the sample is appropriately constituted.

Initially the questionnaire was completed virtually in 2017 by 264 participants. The same instructional manipulation checks described in the previous chapter were employed in this study as well. Fifty-three cases were deleted as a result of inaccurate responses to the two items, thus resulting in a final sample size of N=211 managers. Though this may be seen as a moderately sized sample by the standards of most social survey research, the fact that all of the participants in the sample are managers—a niche and difficult to reach population—suggests that it is relatively large.

Respondents provided informed consent prior to participation in the research. They were first asked for some basic demographic information (years of managerial experience, industry or sector of employment, gender, age, and race) and were then presented immediately with these instructions: "*Imagine that you are recruiting an employee for the most typical role in your organization. We will now show you some photographs of potential job applicants for this role. Assuming that all applicants are roughly equally qualified, how likely would you want the following persons to work for you?"* The respondents then rated the 10 test faces, presented in randomized order (established using a random number table), on a scale of 1 to 7, where 1 means that the respondents are "NOT AT ALL LIKELY" to hire the person depicted in the photograph and 7 means that the respondents are "EXTREMELY LIKELY" to hire the person depicted in the photograph.

Because the focus of this chapter is on discriminatory attitudes towards non-binary job applicants, only cisgendered hiring managers were targeted for inclusion in the sample. For this reason, participant gender was measured in the survey instrument using the traditional binary (0=men, 1=women).

The sample of managers is 55.9 percent female, with an average age of 41.04 years (s.d.=10.51). In aggregate, the respondents reported a mean of 9.49 years of managerial experience, with a standard deviation of 6.98. Employment by industry/sector is as follows: 47.9 percent in the private sector (services), 13.7 percent in the private sector (manufacturing), 28.0 percent in the public sector, and 10.4 percent in the non-profit sector. In terms of racial demographics, 82.9 percent are white, 4.7 percent are black, 3.3 percent are east Asian, 3.3 percent are south Asian, 1.4 percent are American Indian, and 4.3 percent are of mixed race. All participants were located in the United States of America at the time of the research.

**Data Analysis**

In order to evaluate the possibility of employment discrimination against the non-binary, the statistical analyses decompose the employability ratings by *gender fluidity* (gender typical faces vs. GQ25% vs. GQ50% vs. GQ75% vs. GQ100%), *baseline job applicant gender* (originally male vs. originally female) and the *gender of the managerial respondent* (male vs. female), the latter of which was entered into the model as a between-subjects variable. Thus, a $5 \times 2 \times 2$ mixed design analysis of variance (ANOVA), based on the above repeated measures, was modeled, along with potential interaction effects. This quantitative approach to studying sexualities answers Sumerau et al.'s (2017) call for more statistical research in this area.

# RESULTS

Table 4.1 reports the main effects of the experiment. Following Mauchly's test of sphericity (Mauchly's $W=0.788$) and a corresponding Huynh-Feldt correction, there was a main effect of gender fluidity ($F(3.69, 770.44)=18.26$, $p<0.001$, $\eta_p^2=0.08$) where the participants rated the two baseline images highest ($M=4.95$, $SE=0.08$) followed by lower ratings for the 25 percent feminized/masculinized images ($M=4.70$, $SE=0.09$), the 50 percent feminized/masculinized images ($M=4.73$, $SE=0.09$), the 75 percent feminized/masculinized images ($M=4.70$, $SE=0.09$), and the 100 percent feminized/masculinized images ($M=4.64$, $SE=0.09$). These findings are displayed graphically in Figure 4.2. There was also a main effect of baseline job applicant gender ($F(1, 209)=11.98$, $p=0.001$, $\eta_p^2=0.05$), where the five originally male faces were rated higher ($M=4.81$, $SE=0.09$) than the five originally female faces ($M=4.68$, $SE=0.09$). Respondent gender was not found to be statistically significant in the main effects model, suggesting that there was no difference in main effects ratings between male and female managers.

Further pairwise statistics (Bonferroni-corrected) were subsequently analyzed post-hoc. Simple contrasts of both the baseline male and female faces were made, separately, with the four increasingly feminized faces as well as the four increasingly masculinized faces. The baseline faces were rated significantly higher than: (i) the 25 percent feminized/masculinized images ($F(1, 209)=36.56$, $p<0.001$, $\eta_p^2=0.15$), (ii) the 50 percent feminized/masculinized images ($F(1, 209)=24.91$, $p<0.001$, $\eta_p^2=0.11$), (iii) the 75 percent feminized/masculinized images ($F(1, 209)=39.62$, $p<0.001$, $\eta_p^2=0.16$), and (iv) the 100 percent feminized/masculinized images ($F(1, 209)=45.40$, $p<0.001$, $\eta_p^2=0.18$). In other words, it appears from these results that employers demonstrate a significant preference for gender typical job applicants vis-à-vis the four gender fluid job applicants.

In order to explore the question of whether incremental increases in gender fluidity (feminization and masculinization) are associated with discrete reductions in employability ratings, three separate paired sample t-tests were carried out. A p-value cut-off of 0.02 was used for each of the three t-tests in order to correct for familywise error ($0.05/3=0.02$). No significant differences in ratings were found between the 25 percent feminized/masculinized images and the 50

*Table 4.1  Main effects of the 5×2×2 mixed design ANOVA*

| | Effect type | Mean rating (SE) | Mean rating difference | F | p | $\eta_p^2$ |
|---|---|---|---|---|---|---|
| Gender Fluidity (Gender Typical; GQ25%; GQ50%; GQ75%; GQ100%) | Within-subjects | Gender Typical: 4.95 (0.08)<br>GQ25%: 4.70 (0.09)<br>GQ50%: 4.73 (0.09)<br>GQ75%: 4.70 (0.09)<br>GQ100%: 4.64 (0.09) | GQ25%–Gender Typical=−0.25<br>GQ50%–Gender Typical=−0.22<br>GQ75%–Gender Typical=−0.25<br>GQ100%–Gender Typical=−0.31 | 18.26 | <0.001 | 0.08 |
| Baseline Job Applicant Gender (male; female) | Within-subjects | Male: 4.81 (0.09)<br>Female: 4.63 (0.09) | −0.18 | 11.98 | 0.001 | 0.05 |
| Respondent Gender (male; female) | Between-subjects | Male: 4.78 (0.13)<br>Female: 4.71 (0.12) | −0.07 | 0.198 | 0.66 | 0.00 |

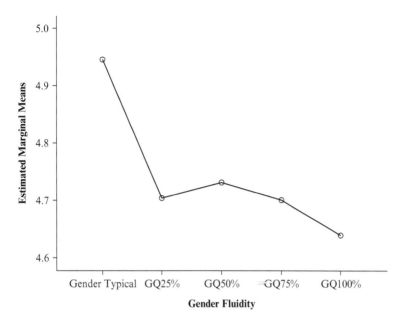

*Notes:*  Gender Typical is the composite of the male and female sexually dimorphic, "average" faces. GQ25% is the composite of the male and female faces that have been altered 25% toward the opposite sex. GQ50% is the composite of the male and female faces that have been altered 50% toward the opposite sex. GQ75% is the composite of the male and female faces that have been altered 75% toward the opposite sex. GQ100% is the composite of the male and female faces that have been altered 100% toward the opposite sex, and are thus androgynous.

*Figure 4.2    Graphical representation of the main effect of gender fluidity*

percent feminized/masculinized images ($t(210)=-0.972$, $p=0.33$, two tailed). No significant differences in ratings were subsequently found between the 50 percent feminized/masculinized images and the 75 percent feminized/masculinized images ($t(210)=0.971$, $p=0.33$, two tailed). Finally, no significant differences in ratings were subsequently found between the 75 percent feminized/masculinized images and the 100 percent feminized/masculinized images ($t(210)=1.57$, $p=0.12$, two tailed). It would therefore appear that the *degree* of gender fluidity is not a significant factor in explaining discrimination against the non-binary.

Following another Huynh-Feldt correction to redress lack of

*Table 4.2    5×2 interaction effect between baseline job applicant gender and gender fluidity*

| Baseline Gender | Gender Fluidity | Mean (SE) |
|---|---|---|
| Male | 0% Genderqueer | 5.15 (0.09) |
| | 25% Genderqueer | 4.72 (0.09) |
| | 50% Genderqueer | 4.77 (0.09) |
| | 75% Genderqueer | 4.72 (0.10) |
| | 100% Genderqueer | 4.67 (0.09) |
| Female | 0% Genderqueer | 4.74 (0.10) |
| | 25% Genderqueer | 4.69 (0.10) |
| | 50% Genderqueer | 4.69 (0.10) |
| | 75% Genderqueer | 4.68 (0.10) |
| | 100% Genderqueer | 4.61 (0.09) |

*Note:*    $F = 9.48$, $p < 0.001$, $\eta_p^2 = 0.04$

sphericity, there was one significant 5×2 interaction effect between gender fluidity and baseline job applicant gender (originally male vs. originally female) ($F(3.12, 233.23) = 9.48$, $p < 0.001$, $\eta_p^2 = 0.04$). Table 4.2 reports the results of this moderating effect. To simplify interpretation of the interaction, Figure 4.3 reports the results graphically. This figure tentatively seems to suggest that the male faces that have been feminized follow a similar pattern to the main effects whereby the gender typical male appears to be rated higher than his four feminized versions. However, the ratings for the gender typical female vis-à-vis the four masculinized versions appear to follow a much less dramatic decrease in employability ratings along the same trajectory. In order to explore this interaction further, separate paired sample t-tests were carried out. It should be noted that, as a result of the inherent complexities of interpreting interaction effects in the context of repeated measures (McClelland and Judd, 1993), and to minimize the possibility of familywise error (Lehmann and Romano, 2005), the male and female baseline faces were compared, separately, with their four gender fluid versions only, for a total of eight separate tests. Accordingly, a p-value cut-off of 0.006 was used to correct for potential familywise error ($0.05/8 = 0.006$).

When the ratings of the male baseline face were compared to the ratings of the 25 percent feminized version, the 50 percent feminized version, the 75 percent feminized version, and the 100 percent femin-

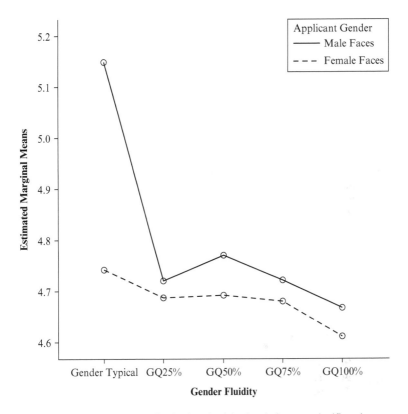

*Notes:* Employability ratings for the four feminized male faces are significantly lower than employability ratings for the gender typical male face. There is no significant difference between the gender typical female face and the four masculinized female faces, although all five female faces are rated lower than the gender typical male face.

*Figure 4.3 Graphical representation of the 5×2 interaction effect between baseline job applicant gender and gender fluidity*

ized version, all paired sample t-tests were found to be statistically significant at the 0.001 level, suggesting a significant preference for the sex-typical male over the feminized versions. When the ratings of the female baseline face were compared with the ratings of the 25 percent masculinized version, the 50 percent masculinized version, the 75 percent masculinized version, and the 100 percent masculinized version, none was found to be statistically significant at the

0.006 cut-off. However, two important points are worth noting. First, the difference between the baseline female face and the 100 percent masculinized version, were it not for the familywise error correction, would have been found to be statistically significant (t(210)=2.07, p=0.04, two tailed). Secondly, as clearly displayed in Figure 4.3, all five of the originally female job applicants were rated, in absolute terms, lower than all five of the corresponding originally male job applicant faces. In other words, the male faces that were feminized suffered the greatest *relative* fall in ratings, but the female faces that were masculinized were rated lowest in *absolute* terms.

## SEXUAL DIMORPHISM IS AN ASSET, BUT ONLY FOR MEN

The results of these analyses suggest that it is difficult, although perhaps not impossible, to escape from the categorizing logic of SIT (Tajfel, 1981; Turner et al., 1987; Sherif, 2015; Hogg, 2016), and, moreover, that sexually dimorphic facial features are an asset when it comes to employability, but apparently only for men. Looking at the big picture, the research points to a propensity towards binary classifications on the part of employers and a preference for sex typicality. The main effects model showed a very clear distinction between the baseline, i.e. gender typical, faces on the one hand, and the feminized and masculinized faces on the other. However, no significant distinction was found between the different *degrees* of feminized and masculinized faces, pointing to the primacy of binary thinking over and above gender fluidity. The same binary pattern of thinking was also found in the interaction effect with regard to comparisons between, on the one hand, the male gender typical face and, on the other, the four increasingly feminized versions, all of which were perceived by the respondents as less employable. No significant differences were found between the gender typical female photo and the masculinized versions of it, but this singularity could potentially be explained by the fact that the respondents might have been contrasting the female test faces with the male test faces, once again returning us to the power of SIT and the primacy of binary categorization.

Looking specifically at the research questions posed above, recall that the first asked whether cisgendered job applicants are rated higher on employability than non-binary job applicants. The main effects model unambiguously confirms that the two gender typical job applicants enjoy higher ratings than their genderqueer counterparts, offering some compelling evidence of employment discrimination against the non-binary that, perhaps, mimics sexual discrimination against the non-binary. The interaction model similarly found that the feminized male applicants suffered from significantly reduced employability vis-à-vis the gender typical male job applicant; however, the masculinized women (after a p-value correction to address potential familywise error) were not rated significantly different from the gender typical female applicant. In other words, it appears to be *relatively* more disadvantageous for one to present as a feminized man than as a masculinized woman in the labor market, although, on the whole, the masculinized females were, overall, rated lower in *absolute* terms than even the feminized males.

The second research question asked whether increasing levels of feminization of male applicants, and increasing levels of masculinization of female applicants, are associated with incrementally reduced employability evaluations. In the main effects model, the four degrees of gender fluidity (GQ25%, GQ50%, GQ75%, and GQ100%) decreased employability ratings equally vis-à-vis the baseline faces, so it does not appear that gradually increasing levels of masculinization/feminization further reduce one's chances of success in the labor market. Alternatively stated, it would seem that employers discriminate against all non-binary applicants, regardless of the degree to which they present in a job interview as gender fluid.

The third research question asked whether cisgendered male and female hiring managers discriminate against non-binary applicants differently. The results suggest, across both the main effects model and the interaction effect, that male and female managers provided roughly equivalent ratings of the applicants. That is, where discrimination against the non-binary community is taking place in the labor market, both male and female hiring managers are equally discriminatory. This finding is perhaps rather surprising given that women are, like non-binary people, also subject to significant employment discrimination, as evidenced by research on the gender pay gap (Weichselbaumer and Winter-Ember, 2005).

Paradoxically, the results reported in this chapter both confirm and challenge existing literatures on gender discrimination in employment. On the one hand, the findings run *somewhat* counter to one particular strand of feminist literature. For example, some scholars (e.g., Nguyen, 2008) have argued that "butch" women (especially lesbians) are an oppressed and marginalized social group that struggles to resist the judgment of hetero-normative culture (Eves, 2004). Within this literature, "female masculinity" (Halberstam, 1998) is traditionally viewed by men and women as far less desirable than the quintessential "female femininity." But the results presented in this chapter seem to suggest that, at least relative to feminized men, masculinized women do not suffer quite so precipitous a drop in labor market value vis-à-vis gender typical female job applicants. Indeed, after a p-value adjustment for familywise error, the gender typical female was rated no differently than its masculinized versions.

Yet, on the other hand—and it is on this basis that the results can be said to be paradoxical—the findings also confirm feminist literatures pointing to discrimination against women in the labor market and in favor of the position of men. The results are consistent with Acker (1990) and Dougherty and Hode (2016) in that they support the widespread view that femininity is perceived to be *bad* and masculinity as *good*, or at least as relatively *better* than femininity. This generalized status hierarchy is deeply embedded into Western societies (Walby, 1990), and is clearly evident in the data. In the analyses, the gender typical male job applicant was, by far, the highest rated face. It was rated significantly higher than: (i) the four feminized versions of itself, (ii) the four masculinized versions of the baseline female job applicant and (iii) the gender typical female job applicant. Moreover, both the male and female hiring managers expressed a strong preference for the gender typical male applicant over all of the other job applicants. Employment, it seems, may be a playground for sexually dimorphic "masculine men," but everyone else appears to struggle to assert their value in the labor market, at least based on looks alone.

By way of concluding, several limitations of the results reported in this chapter are worth noting, each of which lends itself to a direction for future research. First, the results derive from a survey-based method, and so it is sensible to suggest that the research design should be complemented by case study research in more naturalistic settings. Second, because of the study design, this research is restricted to reporting on the perceptions of managers, but does not take into account the unique experiences of non-binary job applicants. Future studies should therefore seek to look at the experience of discrimination on the part of non-binary people, ideally through the use of qualitative methods. This might involve an ethnography that gives an important voice to people who present as non-binary. Third, though the multivariate nature of the research design is a real strength of this study, it is possible that there are several variables, not measured here, that may well moderate the relationships. For example, future researchers could examine the question of whether the sexual orientation of the managers impacts on their evaluations of the non-binary.

# 5. The effect of facial (a)symmetry on employment chances: smarter, healthier, sexier, more productive?

There is an established psychological literature looking at the positive effects of facial symmetry on sexual selection and mate preference (see Grammer and Thornhill, 1994; Rhodes et al., 1998; Perrett et al., 1999). These effects are based, in large part, on the underlying assumption that a more symmetrical face may be a cue to genetic quality (Scheib et al., 1999), as well as intelligence (Prokosch et al., 2005). In spite of the fact that facial symmetry is one of the most studied physical features in psychological face perception research, its impact in more applied settings, such as employment decision-making, has been largely neglected, with most researchers instead choosing to focus on how "attractiveness," more broadly conceived, impacts on one's employability (Luxen and van de Vijver, 2006) or pay (Fruhen et al., 2015). This is a significant lacuna in the extant literature given the repeated calls for more research linking human physiology, biology and organizations (Heaphy and Dutton, 2008; Nofal et al., 2018), and that both attractiveness (Warhurst and Nickson, 2007; Tews et al., 2009; Gatta, 2011) as well as intelligence, or "general mental ability" (Hunter and Schmidt, 1996; Schmidt and Hunter, 1998; Behling, 1998), are already widely recognized to be vital determinants of one's labor market success. This chapter throws a unique light on the question of whether job applicants with more asymmetric facial features are perceived by managers to be less employable than applicants with more symmetrical faces, and, if so, how this finding might be related to wider perceptions of attractiveness, health, and intelligence.

By specifically focusing on the effects of facial (a)symmetry on job applicant employability, the chapter moves the behavioral science of employee selection and assessment in a new and exciting direction. Whilst there are several studies that look at the effects of attractiveness on recruitment and selection (Beehr and Gilmore, 1982; Morrow, 1990; Chiu and Babcock, 2002) and promotion decision-making (Buunk et al., 2016), these studies do not specifically test for the effects of facial asymmetry and, moreover, they do not consider the evolutionary view that managers' brains may be, in light of our experiences in the ancestral environment, hard-wired, or predisposed, towards favoring people with symmetrical faces. Even research that, like this one, deliberately links employee selection with mate selection via evolutionary theory, has not specifically manipulated facial symmetry in order to unpack its effects (Luxen and van de Vijver, 2006). Thus, this chapter adds something new to what we already know about the relationship between physical appearance and labor market success (or failure).

In the next section, the relevant aspects of evolutionary psychology are reviewed in order to lay the conceptual groundwork for the study. After that, previous literatures from employee selection and assessment and evolutionary psychology are summarized and hypotheses developed. The research methods by which the data were collected and analyzed are then presented. The results are then reported and subsequently discussed.

## DARWIN'S FINCHES AND HUMAN FACES

As we discussed in the first chapter of this book, the roots of evolutionary psychology can be traced back in time to *The Origin of Species* (Darwin, [1859] 1998), arguably the most important text in the biological sciences. Whilst evolutionary biology emphasizes adaptation, natural selection, and the survival of the genotype, evolutionary psychology focuses in contrast on the cognitive and behavioral mechanisms, couched in one's genetic make-up (Dawkins, 1976), that enable (or retard) survival, and that ultimately derive from the challenges that our ancestors faced in a competitive and often dangerous environment (Barkow et al., 1992; Buss, 1995, 2005).

Evolutionary psychology, it has been argued thus far, posits that human behavior and decision-making are driven by neural mechanisms that have evolved over time to help us identify threats to survivability and to "sort" mates for purposes of sexual selection.

The prevailing view of attractiveness, from this perspective, is that physiological and genotypic traits, such as facial symmetry (among many others), are recognizable "signals" of mate quality (Rhodes, 2006). Symmetrical faces are thus viewed as important visual cues to genetic health, intelligence, or what might be referred to as a general fitness factor (Prokosch et al., 2005). Our aesthetic preferences in relation to physical appearance are, in this light, much less about the philosophical nature of beauty (Kant, 1951), and much more about the extent to which phenotypic traits are perceived to enable survival in the struggle for life.

Following Luxen and van de Vijver's (2006) pioneering study, this chapter argues that these hard-wired preferences for mates who present as facially symmetrical may have become generalized beyond our primitive sexual impulses and into the realm of employee selection decision-making. In other words, phenotypes signaling genetic quality may be perceived as "attractive" not only to mates, but also to employers. Support for this parallel can be found in the fact that ill-health, disability, and reduced cognitive ability (e.g., IQ) are all negatively associated with perceived employability (Gottfredson, 1997; Koser et al., 1999; Gouvier et al., 2003). Indeed, further support can be found in extant studies that have shown that sexual attractiveness has also been proved to be a very strong asset for job applicants, and particularly for women (Warhurst and Nickson, 2009; Hakim, 2011). This potential "transmutation" of our values and preferences, from sexual selection to the realm of employee selection, cannot, however, be assumed and, therefore, requires rigorous empirical testing. To this end, the purpose of this chapter is to explain employee selection as a potential function of evolutionary psychological preferences for symmetrical faces.

## ATTRACTIVE AND EMPLOYABLE?

This section briefly reviews two bodies of literature and establishes the study's hypotheses. In the first sub-section, the evolutionary psychology literature in respect to the relationship between facial (a)symmetry and attractiveness, health, and intelligence is synthesized. Next, in the second sub-section, the extant literature on the physical and aesthetic determinants of job applicants' perceived employability is reviewed.

## The Evolutionary Psychology of Facial (A)symmetry

The prevailing view among most—though not all—evolutionary psychologists is that more symmetrical facial features are salient indicators of an increased chance of survivability and reproducibility. Three correlates of facial symmetry have emerged in the literature: (i) attractiveness, (ii) health, and (iii) intelligence, although there is some debate about how strongly correlated facial symmetry is to each factor (e.g., Foo et al., 2017).

Over the last few decades, evidence has accumulated pointing to an empirical association between facial symmetry and perceived attractiveness, and, as a corollary, between asymmetry and unattractiveness (Grammer and Thornhill, 1994; Rhodes et al., 1998; Mealey et al., 1999; Perrett et al., 1999; Little et al., 2001; Penton-Voak et al., 2001; Rhodes et al., 2001a; Rhodes, 2006). Studies such as these suggest that beauty is not exclusively a culturally determined phenomenon, but rather may have something to do with human perceptions of "developmental stability," of which facial symmetry is just one of many proxies, albeit an important one. The argument in this regard is that we may well be sexually attracted to potential mates with symmetrical faces because they appear to maximize the probability that our offspring will survive. To understand this preference, though, it is necessary to also look at the empirical associations between, on the one hand, facial symmetry and, on the other, perceived health and intelligence.

Firstly, with a few notable exceptions (Pound et al., 2014; Jones, 2018), evolutionary psychologists have generally agreed that facial symmetry may be associated with improved health outcomes and, as a corollary, that asymmetry may similarly be associated with a reduced quality of health. A number of scholars have corroborated the link between facial symmetry and health, including Jones et al. (2001), Rhodes et al. (2001b), Zaidel et al. (2005), and Fink et al. (2006), although it should be noted that there is perhaps more evidence for an association between facial symmetry and *perceived* health than *actual* health (Kalick et al., 1998; Shackelford and Larsen, 1999; Foo et al., 2017). The rationale underlying the empirical association between facial symmetry and perceived health is that symmetrical faces may potentially act as a signal of higher genetic quality and pathogen resistance, thus contributing positively to gene propagation.

Secondly, evidence has accumulated over the last few decades of an association between facial symmetry and perceptions of intelligence and, conversely, between facial asymmetry and a perceived lack of intelligence. Zebrowitz et al. (2002) show how facial cues across the life span are correlated with IQ. Prokosch et al. (2005), though focused on body symmetry (as opposed to face symmetry), provide convincing evidence that symmetrical biological features are associated with significantly higher g-loadings on intelligence tests, thus lending evidence to the "general fitness factor" hypothesis. Kanazawa and Kovar (2004) corroborate the argument that fluctuating asymmetry is associated with poor heritability, thus explaining why, in general, beautiful people are more intelligent. Studies such as these provide support for the good genes/bad genes approach to evolutionary psychology, that is, the idea that face symmetry is indicative of good genes, which in turn may also be associated with developmental stability and, again, an increased chance of success in the struggle for life.

In short, some evidence exists—contested though it may be—that people with symmetrical facial features sit at the top of the sexual selection hierarchy. The reason for their superior position as potential mates is that they are generally perceived as more attractive, healthy, and intelligent compared to their facially asymmetrical counterparts. But the question still remains: is this preference transmutable to employer preferences in the context of employee selection and assessment?

**Attractiveness and Employee Selection**

Although there are some studies looking at nonverbal cues to attractiveness in the workplace (Johnson et al., 2010; Lee et al., 2015; Bonaccio et al., 2016), there is no previous work examining the effects of facial (a)symmetry on perceived employability. As a result of this lacuna, the studies reviewed in this sub-section are drawn largely from the wider literatures surrounding the effects of (un)attractiveness on employment decision-making. It is assumed throughout that facial symmetry can serve as a useful proxy for attractiveness, as established above.

Though more concerned with labor market success than employability *per se*, economists such as Hamermesh and Biddle (1993), Mobius and Rosenblat (2006), and Hamermesh (2013) have extensively researched the wage premiums enjoyed by "the good looking." However, unlike the present study, none of these has operational-ized attractiveness and/or unattractiveness by manipulating job applicant facial symmetry. The same limitation also applies to the organizational psychologists and HR scholars who have previously researched how attractiveness impacts on one's employment chances. For example, Marlowe et al. (1996) used inter-rater agreement in order to operationalize attractiveness and found evidence of gender biases. Hosoda et al.'s (2003) meta-analysis found a significant positive relationship between attractiveness and several job-related outcomes across 62 studies. Luxen and van de Vijver (2006), identi-fied throughout this book as a closely aligned study to the aims of this monograph, employed evolutionary theory to explain employ-ers' preferences for attractive job applicants, but, again, they did not specifically test the effect of facial (a)symmetry. Scholarship in the field of HRM has similarly found that hiring managers demonstrate a preference for attractive applicants (Chiu and Babcock, 2002), although this preference appears to vary by gender (Paustian-Underdahl and Slattery Walker, 2015).

The concept of "aesthetic labor" (Nickson et al., 2001; Warhurst and Nickson, 2007; Timming, 2016) provides yet another useful framework for thinking about the role of (un)attractiveness in the workplace. Focusing primarily, though not exclusively, on interactive services (Warhurst et al., 2000), aesthetic labor researchers investigate the employment, monitoring and/or training of job applicants and employees in order that they appeal to customers' visual and aural senses. Within this context, it is argued that hiring managers make "blink decisions" that are based on first impressions of whether or not a job applicant "looks good" (Gatta, 2011). Job applicants pos-sessing the "right looks" can therefore make a positive contribution to the organization's image, or brand (Pettinger, 2004; Timming, 2017a).

Several previous studies have also pointed to the negative role of stigma in reducing one's perceived employability. For example, Rudolph et al. (2009) provide some compelling evidence that over-weight and obese job applicants are significantly disadvantaged in the labor market compared to those of a healthy body mass index. Timming (2015) and Timming et al. (2017) show how job appli-cants with visible tattoos can potentially face serious discrimination in employment interviews. Madera and Hebl (2012) found that hiring managers rated facially stigmatized job applicants lower than non-facially stigmatized job applicants, and also recalled fewer facts about the employment interview as a result of the increased attention paid to the stigma.

In sum, although economists, psychologists, HR scholars, and sociologists have written extensively about the positive effects of attractiveness in the workplace, no one has specifically investigated whether facial asymmetry, as a proxy for unattractiveness, can potentially reduce perceptions of employability. In light of the evolutionary psychology literature cited above, the first hypothesis in this chapter is now presented:

*H1:*    *Job applicants with asymmetrical faces are rated lower on per-ceived employability than job applicants with symmetrical faces.*

Furthermore, because there is also evidence that women are sub-jected to greater appearance-based discrimination compared to men (Wolf, 1991; Warhurst and Nickson, 2009; Hakim, 2011; Paustian-Underdahl and Slattery Walker, 2015), a second hypothesis is also worth testing:

*H2:*    *Facially asymmetrical female job applicants are rated lower in perceived employability than facially asymmetrical male job applicants.*

In the following section, the research methods that were used to test these hypotheses are described.

## RESEARCH METHODS

### Experimental Stimuli

In keeping with the previous two chapters, eight photographs (four men and four women, all Caucasians and of roughly the same facial adiposity and age) were selected as the baseline, or control, group. In order to isolate the impact of facial features (as opposed to skin tone or color, see Chapter 3), black and white photographs of the test faces were used. The photos were selected from a publicly available database of images used in Rhodes et al. (1998), and therefore have already been subjected to manipulation checks and validated. Each face was photographed at a 0° angle, under constant lighting, and with a neutral expression. One hundred and twenty landmark points were strategically placed along the interval features of the face, after which face-morphing software was used to render the eight baseline faces perfectly symmetrical.

The stimulus group was created by using the same face-morphing software to render the eight baseline faces asymmetrical. This manipulation was carried out by increasing the distance between landmark points on one side of the face in order to disrupt symmetry through subtle distortions. Thus, the statistical analysis is based on eight baseline, or symmetrical, faces and eight stimulus, or asymmetrical, faces. For the statistical analyses, composites were created for each group. Because the faces across the two groups are perfectly identical apart from symmetry, any negative impact on employability ratings can be directly attributable to the asymmetrical transformations. Figure 5.1 provides an example of the baseline and stimulus images for one male and one female test face.

These 16 test faces were part of the same sample used in the previous chapter, except different variables are used here. Thus, the

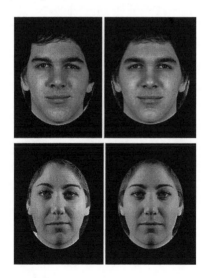

*Source:*   Rhodes et al. (1998)

*Figure 5.1    Example of male and female stimulus (asymmetrical, left) images and baseline (symmetrical, right) images*

participants viewed a total of 26 faces (these 16, plus the 10 sexual dimorphic transforms) in this experiment. Data from the 10 sexual dimorphic faces are reported in the previous chapter).

**Data Collection**

In order to approximate real-world conditions in the experiment and in keeping with the methodologies of the previous chapters, only respondents currently employed as managers were targeted for inclusion. Qualtrics Panels (QP) were employed in order to source a sample of practicing managers. In other words, excluded from the sample is anyone not currently employed in a managerial position. As noted previously, QP draws from a national database of respondents located in the United States of America and applies strict quality control procedures, for example, screening and attention checks, in order to ensure that the sample is appropriately constituted.

The questionnaire was completed online in 2017 by 264 participants. The same instructional manipulation checks (Oppenheimer et al., 2009) used in the previous chapters were built into the experiment to ensure that the respondents were reading the instructions and items carefully. Recall that one item asked respondents to answer a simple arithmetic problem $(7+3)$, and the other listed out 11 hobbies and asked respondents to select the two starting with the letter "r" (rugby and reading). Fifty-three cases were deleted as a result of inaccurate responses to these two items, thus resulting in a final sample size of $N=211$. It should be noted that this is a large sample relative to other studies that similarly use face perception methods (e.g., Belot, 2015).

Respondents provided informed consent prior to participation in the research. Recall that they were first asked for some basic demographic information (years of managerial experience, industry or sector of employment, gender, age, and race) and then presented with the following instructions:

> *Imagine that you are recruiting an employee for the most typical role in your organization. We will now show you some photographs of potential job applicants for this role. Assuming that all applicants are roughly equally qualified, how likely would you want the following persons to work for you?*

Because these instructions are not specific to a given role, the results can be interpreted as general perceptions toward the facial features of the job applicants. The respondents were then asked to rate the 16 test faces, alongside the 10 gender (a)typical faces, presented in randomized order, on a scale of 1 to 7, where 1 means the respondent is "NOT AT ALL LIKELY" to hire this person and 7 means the respondent is "EXTREMELY LIKELY" to hire this person.

The final sample is 55.9 percent female, with an average age of 41.04 years (s.d.=10.51 years). In aggregate, the 211 respondents report a mean of 9.49 years of managerial experience, with a standard deviation of 6.98 years. The participants reported their employment by industry/sector as follows: 47.9 percent were employed in the private sector (services), 13.7 percent were employed in the private sector (manufacturing), 28.0 percent were employed in the public sector, and 10.4 percent were employed in the non-profit sector. In terms of racial demographics, 82.9 percent are white, 4.7 percent are black, 3.3 percent are east Asian, 3.3 percent are south Asian, 1.4 percent are American Indian, and 4.3 percent are mixed race. All participants were located in the United States of America at the time of the data collection.

**Data Analysis**

Prior to the data analysis, composite variables were constructed by averaging scores across the male and female test faces. These composites were then re-scaled to the original 7-point Likert. The statistical analyses decompose employability ratings by *face symmetry* (symmetrical vs. asymmetrical), *sex of face* (male vs. female) and *sex of managerial respondent* (male vs. female), the latter of which was entered into the model as the only between-subjects variable. Thus, a 2×2×2 mixed design ANOVA was modeled.

# RESULTS

Table 5.1 reports the main effects model for perceptions of employability. There was a statistically significant main effect of facial (a)symmetry, with managers rating symmetrical faces (M=4.55, SE=0.07) higher on employability than asymmetrical faces (M=4.26, SE=0.07; $F(1,209)=67.55$, $p<0.001$, $\eta_p^2=0.244$, Cohen's $d=0.286$).

There was also a main effect of sex of face, with the managers rating the male job applicants (M=4.31, SE=0.07) significantly

Table 5.1 Main effects of perceived employability ratings: 2×2×2 mixed design ANOVA

| | Effect type | Mean rating (SE) | Mean rating difference | F | p | $\eta_p^2$ |
|---|---|---|---|---|---|---|
| Face Symmetry (symmetrical; asymmetrical) | Within-subjects | Symmetrical: 4.55 (0.07) Asymmetrical: 4.26 (0.07) | 0.29 | 67.55 | 0.00 | 0.24 |
| Sex of Face (male; female) | Within-subjects | Male: 4.31 (0.07) Female: 4.50 (0.07) | −0.19 | 21.59 | 0.00 | 0.09 |
| Gender of Manager (male; female) | Between-subjects | Male: 4.38 (0.10) Female: 4.43 0(.09) | −0.05 | 1.21 | 0.73 | 0.00 |

lower on employability than the female job applicants (M=4.50, SE=0.07; F(1,222)=21.59, p<0.001, $\eta_p^2$=0.094, Cohen's $d$=0.196).

The gender of the respondent was not found to be statistically significant as a main effect, suggesting that the male and female managers did not differ significantly in their ratings of employability across the test faces.

There were no statistically significant interaction effects to report involving variations in facial symmetry.

On the basis of these results, H1 is confirmed and H2 is rejected. Job applicants with asymmetrical facial features appear to face significant discrimination in employment decision-making compared to job applicants with symmetrical facial features. However, there is no evidence that female job applicants with asymmetrical faces are rated any lower on employability than male job applicants with asymmetrical faces.

These results were subjected to some robustness checks. In order to explore the extent to which the results might vary by sector of employment, the mixed design model was reproduced, separately, for those participants employed in the services sector (N=101), the manufacturing sector (N=29) and the public sector (N=59). It should be noted that separate sensitivity analyses were not possible for the respondents working in the non-profit sector due to the fact that there were only two male participants in this group. All three supplemental models reproduced the results of the full model in relation to facial (a)symmetry. That is, managers in the services sector, the manufacturing sector, and the public sector all expressed a preference for job applicants with symmetrical faces over those with asymmetrical faces. Across the three sensitivity analyses, the only statistically significant moderation involving symmetry was a three-way interaction (face symmetry*sex of face*respondent sex) found in the manufacturing sector. Further decomposition of this interaction effect was not possible due to the small number of cases involved.

## WHAT IS SYMMETRICAL IS GOOD

The results reported in this chapter suggest that job applicants with more asymmetrical facial features are likely to encounter labor market discrimination that is attributable to their appearance (Warhurst et al., 2009). The main effects model revealed, *ceteris paribus*, a significant preference on the part of employers for job applicants that present with symmetrical faces. This preference for symmetrical faces held constant even when the analyses were reproduced across the services sector, manufacturing sector, and public sector managers. The fact that this main effect was found to be significant suggests the finding is robust, especially in the light of the myriad of factors that can also play into labor market outcomes (Heckman et al., 2006). It is also consistent with previous research on the effect of facial asymmetry (Rhodes, 2006; Komori et al., 2009; Jones, 2018).

Experimental research designs, such as this one and others presented in this book, are very useful when it comes to establishing that there are significant differences between stimuli, but they are perhaps less useful in explaining *why* those differences exist. We now know that employers in the United States have a preference for job applicants with symmetrical faces, but we still do not know exactly why they have this disposition. To be sure, this question cannot be answered definitively through a statistical test, and so requires some abstract thinking to shine a light on the possible theoretical mechanism that may be at play here.

As suggested throughout this book, evolutionary psychologists may be able to offer a potential solution to this puzzle. They argue that we value characteristics in others that (appear to) enable our success in propagation and reproduction (Buss, 1995, 2005). Our preferences, and even impulses, are thus governed by a deep-seated need to associate pro-actively with anyone who can arguably increase our chances of survival. As a matter of pre-cognitive instinct, then, we may seek out others whom we perceive to be healthy and intelligent. Similarly, both of these traits may play into our perceptions of attractiveness and sexual selection. Evolutionary theory can thus explain not only who we find attractive, but also why we find them attractive.

On this basis, one potential explanation of the findings reported in this chapter is that our evolutionary preferences are perhaps somehow "transmutable" from the realm of sexual selection and assessment into the realm of personnel selection and assessment. By this is meant that the pre-cognitive drivers of our choice of potential mates may "spill over" into employers' hiring decisions. In other words, just as we are sexually attracted to those we perceive to be healthy and intelligent, so are employers similarly attracted to job applicants that they perceive to be healthy and intelligent. To the extent that facial symmetry is a cue to vitality, cognitive ability, and pathogen resistance, those who present as facially asymmetrical may be unlucky in both love and employment.

**Contribution to the Literature**

This is the first ever experiment to test the effect of facial (a)symmetry on perceived employability, so its empirical contribution to knowledge is already firmly established. But it also makes a theoretical contribution inasmuch as it adds a new dimension to the extant literature on the role of (un)attractiveness in shaping individual employment outcomes. As articulated above, several economists (Hamermesh and Biddle, 1993; Mobius and Rosenblat, 2006; Hamermesh, 2013), psychologists (Marlowe et al., 1996; Hosoda et al., 2003; Luxen and van de Vijver, 2006; Fruhen et al., 2015), sociologists (Nickson et al., 2001; Warhurst and Nickson, 2007), and human resource management researchers (Chiu and Babcock, 2002; Paustian-Underdahl and Slattery Walker, 2015) have already investigated at length the burden of unattractiveness on employment outcomes, but no previous study, until this one, has used photographic asymmetry transformations as a proxy. Another novel theoretical contribution of the present study is that it employs evolutionary psychology to explain *why* employers might prefer symmetric facial features over and above asymmetrical features.

**Practical Implications**

In terms of practical implications for employees and job seekers, it would seem that there is little that can be done to remedy an asymmetrical face. Cosmetic surgery may be able to alter facial aesthetics to some extent, but it is unlikely to be able to align one's eyes so that they appear symmetrical. Similarly, make-up may be used to accentuate facial symmetry, but even then, there are some limits to its ability to conceal blatantly asymmetrical features. Perhaps a more important question than "What is to be done?" is "Why should job applicants have to do anything in the first place?" Essentially, this study has shone a new light on a previously unexplored form of employment discrimination. If the physical configuration of one's face is no different than the color of one's skin (in that both are genetically determined), then we might reasonably ask why both forms of discrimination are not roundly condemned.

For this reason, it is perhaps more appropriate to think about the practical implications of this research for managers and organizations. What steps can they take to minimize the chances of discrimination based on physical appearance (Warhurst et al., 2009)? The results of this study may point to the importance of implementing an effective unconscious bias training program (Noon, 2018), as will be discussed at length in the following chapter. Another positive step in the right direction might involve raising public awareness of the importance of face equality (Changing Faces, 2018). In any event, more needs to be done to reduce or eliminate discrimination that is, in effect, genetically determined.

**Limitations and Directions for Future Research**

The research reported in this chapter benefits from the use of an impressive sample of managers and photographic stimuli that have been previously validated (Rhodes et al., 1998), but there are still several notable limitations, many of which segue into directions for future research. Firstly, the results of this study speak to *perceptions* of employability, and not *actual* labor market outcomes. As noted previously, a field study of the effect of facial asymmetry on actual employability would be ideal, but it would be extremely difficult, if not impossible, to fully isolate the effect from potential confounds. Second, the usual disclaimers associated with the generalizability of experimental designs apply. Though experiments are strong on internal validity, they can give rise to order effects. Thus, it makes sense to replicate this experiment using either a different randomized order of the stimuli or a between-subjects design. Third, although the results show that managers prefer job applicants with symmetrical facial features, the explanation given for this preference is, at present, just a theory. Future research would do well to test this theory by, for example, asking managers to rate job applicants not only on employability, but also on perceived health, intelligence, and attractiveness. With such a design, one could test whether these evolutionary factors moderate, or mediate, the relationship between facial symmetry and perceived employability.

In conclusion, the results reported in this chapter should have wide appeal, given that no one can be said to have a perfectly symmetrical face. The chapter draws welcome attention to a new, previously unexplored, form of employment discrimination based on the shape and physical contours of one's face. It was found that employers are averse to job applicants with asymmetrical faces and it was further suggested that evolutionary psychology may be able to explain the aversion. If job applicants are unsuccessful in a job interview in part because of their facial structure, such discrimination would seem to be just as concerning as discrimination based on other genetic features, such as skin color or indeed gender.

# 6. Unconscious bias and the future of HRM decision-making

Though it may be hard to detect at first glance, a subtle pattern has emerged throughout this book. In short, much of what goes on in the workplace occurs at an unconscious, or, perhaps more accurately, at a sub-conscious level. In other words, organizational behavior can be said to be driven at least in part by our *implicit* cognitive orientations. That is to say, our behavior at work is partially governed by our instincts and impulses, many of which have been shaped by natural selection over millennia. For example, when employers (or indeed potential mates, for that matter) discriminate against people with asymmetrical facial features, sexually atypical faces, or lighter skin tones, they may not be paying *explicit* attention to these traits. Similarly, when employees engage in mobbing behavior against a colleague, they may not recognize it as such because they are being driven not by their socialized selves, but rather by their biological selves. Thus, in the same way that humans breathe without thinking about the act of respiration, we can also discriminate against others without being fully aware of our prejudices and biases. To this end, the aim of this concluding chapter is to explore the role of unconscious bias in the context of human resource management decision-making.

Indeed, human resource managers who genuinely believe that they do not discriminate in employment decision-making are really only fooling themselves for two reasons. First, all "sorting" of employees and/or job applicants—for example, in the performance management or recruitment and selection processes—is, effectively, discrimination. When a candidate with 25 years of experience is hired over the one with five years of experience, or when the employee who generated more sales revenue for the company is promoted over the one who generated less, such decisions are inherently discriminatory, but this type of discrimination tends to be, on the whole, socially, morally, and legally sanctioned. The second reason is that what we believe about ourselves—for example, "I am not a racist," "I accept that women can be just as effective leaders as men," or "I believe that unattractive people are just as capable as good looking people"—is oftentimes, paradoxically, at odds with our actions, behaviors, and decisions. The reason for this apparent disconnect between our beliefs, and behaviors that do not correspond to our beliefs, is that we are all "steered," to some degree or another, by our unconscious mind.

The socio-legal ramifications of unconscious biases within organizations have already been thoroughly rehearsed elsewhere (Lee, 2005; Bagenstos, 2007; Ford, 2014); this chapter focuses instead on its evolutionary psychological underpinnings insofar as they intersect with human resource management decision-making. It is argued that, although (most) HR managers *consciously* aim to be objective, fair, and unbiased in their decisions, the inescapable fact is that we are all influenced *unconsciously* by our implicit beliefs (Bertrand et al., 2005; Quillian, 2008) and background assumptions (Garfinkel, 2002; Timming, 2010) about the social world, both of which are characterized by a state of unintentionality. The impact of unconscious biases on employee "sorting" has not previously been explored in any depth. However, it is beginning to be acknowledged as a problem in need of addressing by HR practitioners (Forbes Human Resources Council, 2018).

The key contribution of this chapter to the field of human resource management is that it calls into question the (ironically) implicit belief that HR decision-making is necessarily intentional and wholly under the volition of the HR manager. It provides a more comprehensive framework through which HR processes can be viewed via the lenses of intentionality and unintentionality. As such, it aligns with a wider need for a fundamental re-orientation of the study of HRM inasmuch as the arguments presented here address the deeply flawed assumption that HRM can be best captured by applying a purely "rational choice" approach to decision-making (Mataiske, 2004).

In the next section, some of the most important studies on implicit bias, from an evolutionary psychological and cognitive neuroscientific perspective, are outlined. After that, we take a look at some of the "seen-but-unnoticed" attributes that have the potential to impact unconsciously on HR decisions. The chapter then draws the book to a close by discussing the implications of unconscious bias for the future of HRM research and practice.

# THE EVOLUTIONARY PSYCHOLOGY OF IMPLICIT BIAS

Psychologists typically divide the mind, and therefore the self, into both conscious and unconscious parts (Bargh and Morsella, 2008). The conscious mind is said to be the foundation of the conscious self (Mead, 1967), which is a constellation of one's values, attitudes, beliefs, and preferences, each of which is characterized by a degree of self-awareness. The unconscious mind equally comprises one's values, attitudes, beliefs, and preferences, but these are *implicit* and therefore located "in the shadow" of self-awareness. Crucially, according to Bertrand et al. (2005), one's explicit attitudes may or may not align with one's implicit attitudes.

The idea of an unconscious mind was, for many years, taken-for-granted (especially by Freudian psychologists) in the absence of empirical corroboration. But in a landmark study on the nature of prejudice, Devine (1989: 15) offered some empirical support for the idea that stereotypical attitudes may be an "automatic" response to social cues, concluding, "[i]t would appear that the automatically activated stereotype-congruent or prejudice-like responses have become independent of one's current attitudes or beliefs." The idea that one can be explicitly opposed to prejudice, but implicitly prejudiced, was further supported by the development of the implicit association tests (see Greenwald et al., 1998, 2003; Nosek et al., 2007; also    https://implicit.harvard.edu/implicit/takeatest.html).    These instruments were initially designed for respondents who are either: (i) unwilling to admit to others or (ii) unable to recognize in themselves that they harbor deep-seated prejudices against certain social groups. In respect to (i), imagine the HR manager who simply does not like certain "types" of people (e.g., short, overweight, non-white, foreign, or unattractive, etc.). In respect to (ii), imagine the HR manager who believes him or herself to be impartial and committed to fairness and equality but, deep down, in the recesses of the mind, harbors a set of implicit biases and prejudices against the "other." Crucially, research has shown that unconscious biases, revealed through the implicit association tests, also translate into discriminatory behaviors (McConnell and Leibold, 2001).

The social psychology of implicit bias is based on the idea that we all hold a set of shared "background assumptions" (Garfinkel, 2002; Timming, 2010) about the social world that exist outside the immediate focus of our attention, but that still influence our decision-making, albeit unintentionally. For this reason, *knowing* that it is wrong to discriminate against someone on the basis of, for example, weight, does not safeguard against such discrimination taking place, which may in part explain the prevalence of discrimination against the overweight and obese within the workplace (Rudolph et al., 2009; Levay, 2014; Nickson et al., 2016). Indeed, at least in Western societies, the implicit biases of HR managers may well explain the disproportionate labor market success of those who present as tall, white, healthy, attractive and, of course, male, because characteristics such as these are integral to our normatively constructed "background assumptions" in defining the types of people that we, as a society, consider "desirable" (Jones, 2010).

The evolutionary psychology of implicit bias is supported empirically by a whole raft of complementary studies within the cognitive neurosciences. For example, Phelps et al. (2000) employed functional magnetic resonance imaging (fMRI) to examine the neural functioning of research participants completing the implicit association test on race. They found significant amygdala activation in the subcortical area of the brain (the area that regulates fear), suggesting that behavioral responses are influenced by cultural evaluations that may be buried deep in the unconscious mind. This finding was later supported by another fMRI study (Cunningham et al., 2004), which found similar amygdala activation in white respondents based on short (30 millisecond) exposures to black faces. Richeson et al. (2003) report a similar activation in the dorsolateral prefrontal cortex region of the brain (the part responsible for moral decision-making) among those subjects with the highest levels of implicit bias (according to the implicit association test), once again pointing to the assumption that unconscious attitudes translate into tangible and measurable neurological manifestations. In short, the cognitive neuroscience of unconscious bias provides clear and strong evidence in favor of the existence of implicit bias, and clearly suggests that we are not in complete control over the judgments that we form about others.

The implications of implicit bias for the field of HRM are profound and we have barely scratched the surface in terms of research on this topic (see CIPD, 2014). Several studies have sought to link unconscious bias to employee selection decision-making. For example, Bertrand and Malainathan (2004), in a seminal study in economics, examined implicit bias against job applicants' names, concluding that an "Emily" or "Greg" is significantly more employable than a "Lakisha" or "Jamal." Rooth (2007) further corroborated this finding by carrying out a similar experiment, but one using "Arab" and "Swedish" sounding names in Sweden. McGinnity and Lunn (2011) found that job applicants with native-sounding names were twice as likely to be invited to an interview as those with foreign names. The problem with the extant literature on implicit bias in HR decision-making is that it focuses, overwhelmingly, on obvious racial and ethnic differences (Quillian, 2008). Whilst these studies are certainly important, it has been shown throughout this book that unintentional discrimination in HRM reaches far beyond race and ethnicity into a set of wider, mostly physical attributes possessed by workers. In the next section, we examine some of these attributes in an attempt to make the unconscious conscious.

## MAKING THE UNCONSCIOUS CONSCIOUS?

One of the merits of this book is that it helps to make the unconscious conscious. What exactly does this mean? Readers who have participated in a workplace mob or discriminated against employees and/or job applicants as a result of their physical attributes may now be aware of the nature of their behaviors. This awareness can only be seen as a welcome and positive development in that it may reduce such deleterious behaviors. One of the limitations of this book, however, is that it shines a light on only a handful of these implicit biases. Of course, it is not possible to identify all, or even most, of the physiological attributes that can leave a positive (or a negative) impression on the unconscious mind, especially in the context of employee "sorting." Indeed, the fact that such attitudes are implicit, and thus "in the shadow" of one's consciousness, makes them difficult to uncover.

We have already seen how those who present with asymmetrical facial features suffer significant discrimination in the labor market, alongside those with whiter, paler skin as well as those who present as sex atypical. We have already seen how evolutionary psychology can explain these physiological preferences. But there is a myriad of other features that could also reduce one's job chances. A few of them are described below.

## Height

Body height has been roundly associated with a number of important life outcomes. For example, it has been found that, among adolescents, shorter boys (and girls) are statistically significantly less likely to have romantic relationships in comparison to their taller counterparts (Cawley et al., 2006). Schultz (2002) and Persico et al. (2004) illustrate empirically that taller people receive a significant wage premium vis-à-vis their shorter counterparts, whilst Lindqvist (2012) shows how height is positively related to the attainment of leadership positions in the workplace. The logic underlying what might be called "heightism" is evolutionary. That is, it could be argued, and indeed has been argued (Blaker et al., 2013), that taller people possess a labor market advantage because they are perceived as more dominant, healthy, and intelligent. Alternatively stated, shorter people are seen as less likely to survive and thrive in a competitive environment.

Although previous work has found a strong and positive correlation between height and income (Schultz, 2002; Persico et al., 2004; Judge and Cable, 2004), the effect of height on HR decision-making (which is, obviously, a proxy for income) has not been explored to any great extent. However, based on Lindqvist's (2012) research illustrating that managers are, *ceteris paribus*, taller than non-supervisory employees, it can be assumed that recruiters are generally taller than most job applicants, arguably creating a fertile ground for unconscious bias on the basis of height in recruitment and selection and perhaps also performance management. Further research, however, is needed on the effect of height on employment decision-making as well as outcomes.

## Weight

There is a plethora of evolutionary psychological studies regarding the negative effects of adiposity (that is, body weight) on, for example, perceptions of attractiveness and health (Singh and Young, 1995; Coetzee et al., 2009; Rantala et al., 2013). In general, people who are significantly overweight (and also significantly underweight) are perceived more negatively in society than people who are characteristically slim and fit. In the specific case of overweight and obesity, these perceptions are often driven by the stereotyping of adiposity wherein excess weight is associated with implicit perceptions of laziness, stupidity, and a lack of motivation (Schwartz et al., 2003).

Unlike with height, there has been considerable research on the effects of adiposity on workplace "sorting" (Levay, 2014). For example, Pingitore et al. (1994) found that overweight job applicants suffered from weight-based bias in an experimental job interview. The effect was particularly pronounced when the rater reported satisfaction with his or her own body image. Larkin and Pines (1979) found that, *ceteris paribus*, "fat persons" are less highly rated than normal-weight job applicants in relation to employability. Klesges et al. (1990) found that obese job applicants were not only perceived to be less qualified than non-obese applicants, but were also significantly less likely to be hired. Finkelstein et al. (2007) similarly concluded that excess weight is negatively associated with hireability ratings, amongst several other work-related outcomes. These consistent findings are reflected in a recent meta-analysis by Rudolph et al. (2009), which points to adiposity as a major source of bias and prejudice (Crandal, 1994) in the workplace.

In spite of this huge body of research, no one has explored the effects of adiposity on employability from the viewpoint of unconscious or implicit bias. It is clear that employee sorting is impacted by job applicants' and employees' body mass, but it is, as yet, unclear how much of the decision-making process is driven by HR managers' conscious and unconscious prejudices against the overweight and obese. To further complicate matters, weight, in and of itself, is not a legally protected category in employment law (*Human Resource Management International Digest*, 2006), therefore, there is no immediate sanction against weight-based discrimination in the workplace unless it intersects with disability. In any event, further research is needed on the evolutionary psychology of weight-based discrimination in the labor market.

**Accent and Pitch**

Of course, not all unconscious bias is driven by visible cues. One's voice can be an equally powerful auditory source of potential discrimination. Neuro- and socio-linguists, for example, have examined accent in terms of foreign versus native intonation, as well as different regional dialects within countries. Researchers have found that accents are strong cues to one's social class affiliation (Mugglestone,

2007), with such perceptions being especially prominent in England (Hughes et al., 2012). Moreover, the pitch of (male) voices has also been found to be a cue to one's sexual orientation (Smyth et al., 2003), as well as also prejudicing one's chances of success in a job interview (Bell et al., 2011). The evolutionary explanation of this bias again can be traced back to perceived dominance in the social hierarchy.

A number of studies have examined the effect of speech on one's employability, though none of these, as yet, has examined utterances from the perspective of unconscious bias. Timming (2017b) conducted a simulated telephone job interview in the U.S. labor market. He found that, with the exception of the English accent, job applicants with foreign accents, and especially women, were rated significantly lower on perceived hireability compared to those with the standard American accent. Foreign accents, he argued, were associated with underdeveloped countries and a lower social class. In a similar vein, Ashley (2010) found that minority ethnic solicitors in the U.K. intentionally altered their accents to upper class English in order to increase the chances of success in the labor market. Relatedly, Warhurst (2016) outlines how speech discrimination by employers often results in working class invisibility in service-dominated labor markets. Studies such as these demonstrate clearly how aural factors can play an important role in relation to unconscious bias in workplace sorting decisions. To be sure, more research is needed on the evolutionary psychology of speech in the workplace.

**Mutable Attributes**

Finally, whilst this book has focused primarily on physiological features, there is any number of additional malleable attributes that can also unconsciously influence HR decision-making. Because of the sheer number and variations of mutable attributes, there is no single body of literature that can be used as a reference point, but several aesthetic dimensions deserve mention. Obviously, the clothing we wear is an important cue to, for example, social class affiliation (Crane, 2000) or religious identity (King and Ahmad, 2010), both of which can signal one's social status. An equally strong source of bias is the adornment of our bodies with features such as tattoos (Timming, 2015, 2017a; Timming and Perrett, 2016, 2017; Baumann et al., 2016; Timming et al., 2017), jewellery (Warhurst et al., 2000), or the application of cosmetics and make-up (Nickson et al., 2005). Even something as innocuous as the presence (or the absence) of facial hair (Muscarella and Cunningham, 1996) can subtly and implicitly influence how job applicants are perceived in the workplace. All of these mutable features deserve further scholarly attention in future research.

## CONCLUSIONS

Biology and human resource management may seem like odd bedfellows, but through the unique lens of evolutionary psychology, they explain, in concert, much more together than they can individually. This is among the first ever monographs on what might be called the evolutionary psychology of human resource management, or "evolutionary HRM," and hopefully it will not be the last. If anything, the analyses presented here have only scratched the surface of the complicated interface between human physiology and organizational behavior. The true test of the integrity of any piece of research is whether it generates more questions than it aimed to answer. Yet another hallmark of good research is its ability to shine a new, and controversial, light on debates that were thought to be old and tired, as described in the first chapter. On both of these measures, only time will tell whether this book has been successful.

One of the key conclusions to be drawn from the book is that, as a field of study, human resource management is not doomed to obsolescence (Dundon and Rafferty, 2018). As shown in this chapter, recent developments in the brain sciences have opened up a new frontier for HRM scholars. As we approach this new frontier, we may have to enhance our methodological toolkits to go beyond surveys and interviews and include heart monitors, brain scanners, blood tests, and genetic screening, among other biological assessors. To be clear, this paradigm shift does *not* at all mean abandoning the traditional social sciences. Although sociology may have emerged from this analysis somewhat beaten and bloodied, it can still offer "value added" in the elusive general theory of people and organizations, or rather people in organizations. But in the absence of a substantial "biological turn"—which this book has sought to hasten—our future understanding of organizational behavior and human resource management decision-making is likely to be not dissimilar to our understanding today.

We are all the products of our animal nature and the environment in which we live and interact. The organization of work is thus necessarily impacted by factors intrinsic and extrinsic to the individual employee. This book has shone a light on just some of those intrinsic factors, arguing that they have developed as a result of natural selection across human history. It is only through understanding of our natural selves that we can proactively structure our environment so as to mitigate against our more destructive instincts.

# References

Abrams, D. and Hogg, M.A. (1998) *Social Identifications: A Social Psychology of Intergroup Relations and Group Processes.* London: Routledge.

Accomazzo, S. (2012) Anthropology of violence: historical and current theories, concepts, and debates in physical and socio-cultural anthropology. *Journal of Human Behavior in the Social Environment* 22: 535–552.

Acker, J. (1990) Hierarchies, jobs, bodies: a theory of gendered organizations. *Gender & Society* 4(2): 139–158.

Adorno, T.W.; Frenkel-Brunswik, E.; Levinson, D.J. and Sanford, R.N. (1950) *The Authoritarian Personality.* Studies in Prejudice Series, American Jewish Committee, New York: Harper.

Allport, G.W. (1954) *The Nature of Prejudice.* Oxford: Addison-Wesley.

Andersson, M. and Simmons, L.W. (2006) Sexual selection and mate choice. *Trends in Ecology and Evolution* 21(6): 296–302.

Aquino, K. and Lamertz, K. (2004) A relational model of workplace victimization: social roles and patterns of victimization in dyadic relationships. *Journal of Applied Psychology* 89: 1023–1034.

Arce, C.H.; Murguia, E. and Frisbie, W.P. (1987) Phenotype and life chances among Chicanos. *Hispanic Journal of Behavioral Sciences* 9(1): 19–32.

Armstrong, N. and Welsman, J. (2001) Peak oxygen uptake in relation to growth and maturation in 11- to 17-year old humans. *European Journal of Applied Physiology* 85(6): 546–551.

Arthur, J.B. (1994) Effects of human resource systems on manufacturing performance and turnover. *Academy of Management Journal* 37(3): 670–687.

Arulampalam, W.; Booth, A.L. and Bryan M.L. (2007) Is there a glass ceiling over Europe? Exploring the gender pay gap across the wage distribution. *Industrial and Labor Relations Review* 60(2): 163–186.

Ashcraft, K.L. and Muhr, S.L. (2018) Coding military command as a promiscuous practice? Unsettling the gender binaries of leadership metaphors. *Human Relations* 71(2): 206–228.

Ashforth, B.E. and Mael, F. (1989) Social identity theory and the organization. *Academy of Management Review* 14(1): 20–39.

Ashley L. (2010) Making a difference? The use (and abuse) of diversity management at the UK's elite law firms. *Work, Employment & Society* 24(4): 711–727.

Bagenstos, S.R. (2007) Implicit bias, "science," and antidiscrimination law. *Harvard Law & Policy Review* 1: 477–493.

Balducci, C.; Alfano, V. and Fraccaroli, F. (2009) Relationships between mobbing at work and MMPI-2 personality profile, post-traumatic stress symptoms, and suicidal ideation and behavior. *Violence and Victims* 24: 52–67.

Balducci, C.; Fraccaroli, F. and Schaufeli, W.B. (2011) Workplace bullying and its relation with work characteristics, personality, and post-traumatic stress symptoms: an integrated model. *Anxiety, Stress, & Coping: An International Journal* 24: 499–513.

Barber, N. (1995) The evolutionary psychology of physical attractiveness: sexual selection and human morphology. *Evolution and Human Behavior* 16: 395–424.

Bargh, J.A. and Morsella, E. (2008) The unconscious mind. *Perspectives on Psychological Science* 3(1): 73–79.

Barkow, J.; Cosmides, L. and Tooby, J. (eds) (1992) *The Adapted Mind: Evolutionary Psychology and the Generation of Culture.* Oxford: Oxford University Press.

Barrett, H.C. (2005) Adaptations to Predators and Prey. In *The Handbook of Evolutionary Psychology* (edited by D.M. Buss). Hoboken: John Wiley & Sons, pp. 200–223.

Baughman, H.M.; Dearing, S.; Giammarco, E. and Vernon, P.A. (2012) Relationships between bullying behaviours and the dark triad: a study with adults. *Personality and Individual Differences* 52: 571–575.

Baumann, C.; Timming, A.R. and Gollan, P. (2016) Taboo tattoos? A study of the gendered effects of body art on consumers' attitudes toward visibly tattooed front-line staff. *Journal of Retailing and Consumer Services* 29: 31–39.

Baumeister, R.F.; Smart, L. and Boden, J.M. (1996) Relation of threatened egotism to violence and aggression: the dark side of high self-esteem. *Psychological Review* 103: 5–33.

Becker, B. and Gerhart, B. (1996) The impact of human resource management on organizational performance: progress and prospects. *Academy of Management Journal* 39(4): 779–801.

Becker, W.J. and Cropanzano, R. (2010) Organizational neuroscience: the promise and prospects of an emerging discipline. *Journal of Organizational Behavior* 31(7): 1055–1059.

Becker, W.J.; Cropanzano, R. and Sanfey, A.G. (2011) Organizational neuroscience: taking organizational theory inside the neural black box. *Journal of Management* 37: 933–961.

Beech, N. (2011) Liminality and the practices of identity reconstruction. *Human Relations* 64: 285–302.

Beehr, T.A. and Gilmore, D.C. (1982) Applicant attractiveness as a perceived job-relevant variable in selection of management trainees. *Academy of Management Journal* 25: 607–617.

Beer, M.; Spector, B.; Lawrence, P.; Mills, D.Q. and Walton, R. (1984) *Human Resource Management: A General Manager's Perspective.* New York: Free Press.

Behling, O. (1998) Employee selection: will intelligence and conscientiousness do the job? *Academy of Management Executive* 12: 77–86.

Bell, M.P.; Ozbilgin, M.; Beauregard, T.A. and Surgevil, O. (2011) Voice, silence and diversity in 21st century organizations: Strategies for inclusion of gay, lesbian, bisexual and transgender employees. *Human Resource Management* 50(1): 131–146.

Belot, M. (2015) Cognitive discrimination: A benchmark experimental study. *Journal of Neuroscience, Psychology, and Economics* 8: 173–185.

Bem, S.L. (1981) Gender schema theory: a cognitive account of sex typing. *Psychological Review* 88(4): 354–364.

Berger, P.L. and Luckmann, T. (1966) *The Social Construction of Reality: A Treatise in the Sociology of Knowledge.* New York: Anchor.

Berthelsen, M.; Skogstad, A.; Lau, B. and Einarsen, S. (2011) Do they stay or do they go? A longitudinal study of intentions to leave and exclusion from working life among targets of workplace bullying. *International Journal of Manpower* 32(2): 178–193.

Bertrand, M. and Malainathan, S. (2004) Are Emily and Greg more employable than Lakisha and Jamal? *American Economic Review* 94(4): 991–1013.

Bertrand, M.; Chugh, D. and Mullainathan, S. (2005) Implicit discrimination. *American Economic Review* 95(2): 94–98.

Birdi, K.; Clegg, C.; Patterson, M.; Robinson, A.; Stride, C.; Wall, T. and Wood, S. (2008) The impact of human resource and operational management practices on company productivity: A longitudinal study. *Personnel Psychology* 61(3): 467–501.

Bjørkelo, B. (2013) Workplace bullying after whistleblowing: future research and implications. *Journal of Managerial Psychology* 28: 306–323.

Blaker, N.M.; Rompa, I.; Dessing, I.H.; Vriend, A.F.; Herschberg, C. and van Vugt, M. (2013) The height leadership advantage in men and women: testing evolutionary psychology predictions about the perceptions of tall leaders. *Group Processes & Intergroup Relations* 16(1): 17–27.

Blau, F.D. and Kahn, L.M. (2003) Understanding international differences in the gender pay gap. *Journal of Labor Economics* 21(1): 106–144.

Boddy, C.R. (2011) Corporate psychopaths, bullying and unfair supervision in the workplace. *Journal of Business Ethics* 100: 367–379.

Bohan, J.S. (1993) Regarding gender: essentialism, constructionism, and feminist psychology. *Psychology of Women Quarterly* 17(1): 5–21.

Bonaccio, S.; O'Reilly, J.; O'Sullivan, S.L. and Chiocchio, F. (2016) Nonverbal behavior and communication in the workplace: a review and an agenda for research. *Journal of Management* 42: 1044–1074.

Bonilla-Silva, E. (1996) Rethinking racism: toward a structural interpretation. *American Sociological Review* 62(3): 465–480.

Bowling, N.A. and Beehr, T.A. (2006) Workplace harassment from the victim's perspective: a theoretical model and meta-analysis. *Journal of Applied Psychology* 91: 998–1012.

Branch, S.; Ramsay, S. and Barker, M. (2013) Workplace bullying, mobbing and general harassment: a review. *International Journal of Management Reviews* 15: 280–299.

Brewer, M.B. (1999) The psychology of prejudice: ingroup love and outgroup hate? *Journal of Social Issues* 55(3): 429–444.

Brewis, J.; Hampton, M.P. and Linstead, S. (1997) Unpacking Priscilla: subjectivity and identity in the organization of gendered appearance. *Human Relations* 50(10): 1275–1304.

Brickell, C. (2006) The sociological construction of gender and sexuality. *The Sociological Review* 54(1): 87–113.

Brodsky, C.M. (1976) *The Harassed Worker*. Lexington: Lexington Books.

Browne, J. (1995) *Charles Darwin: Voyaging*. Princeton: Princeton University Press.

Buhrmester, M.; Kwang, T. and Gosling, S.D. (2011) Amazon's mechanical Turk: a new source of inexpensive, yet high-quality, data? *Perspectives on Psychological Science* 6(1): 3–5.

Buss, D.M. (1995) Evolutionary psychology: a new paradigm for psychological science. *Psychological Inquiry*, 6: 1–30.

Buss, D.M. (1997) Human social motivation in evolutionary perspective: grounding terror management theory. *Psychological Inquiry* 8: 22–26.

Buss, D.M. (ed.) (2005) *The Handbook of Evolutionary Psychology*. New York: Wiley.

Buss, D.M. and Shackelford, T.K. (1997) Human aggression in evolutionary psychological perspective. *Clinical Psychology Review* 17: 605–619.

Butler, J. (1990) *Gender Trouble*. London: Routledge.

Butler, J. (1993) *Bodies that Matter: On the Discursive Limits of Sex*. London: Routledge.

Buunk, A.P.; Zurriaga, R.; González-Navarro, P. and Monzani, L. (2016) Attractive rivals may undermine the expectation of career advancement and enhance jealousy: an experimental study. *European Journal of Work and Organizational Psychology* 25: 790–803.

Calderwood, C.; Gabriel, A.S.; Rosen, C.C.; Simon, L.S. and Koopman, J. (2016) 100 years running: the need to understand why employee physical activity benefits organizations. *Journal of Organizational Behavior* 37(7): 1104–1109.

Calhoun, C. (ed) (1994) *Social Theory and the Politics of Identity*. Cambridge: Blackwell.

Campbell, A. (2005) Aggression. In *The Handbook of Evolutionary Psychology* (edited by D.M. Buss). Hoboken: John Wiley & Sons, pp. 628–652.

Cawley, J.; Joyner, K. and Sobal, J. (2006) Size matters: the influence of adolescents' weight and height on dating and sex. *Rationality and Society* 18(1): 67–94.

Changing Faces. (2018) Recruiting a candidate who has a mark, scar or condition which affects their appearance. www.changing faces.org.uk/adviceandsupport/self-help-guides/work/a-guide-for-employers. [Accessed 16 March 2018.]

Charles, C.A.D. (2003) Skin bleaching, self-hate, and black identity in Jamaica. *Journal of Black Studies* 33(6): 711–728.

Chiu, R.K. and Babcock, R.D. (2002) The relative importance of facial attractiveness and gender in Hong Kong selection decisions. *International Journal of Human Resource Management* 13: 141–155.

Christoffersen, M.N. (1994) A follow-up study of long-term effects of unemployment on children: loss of self-esteem and self-destructive behavior among adolescents. *Childhood* 2: 212–220.

Chung, V.Q.; Gordon, J.S.; Veledar, E. and Chen, S.C. (2010) Hot or not—evaluating the effect of artificial tanning on the public's perception of attractiveness. *Dermatologic Surgery* 36(11): 1651–1655.

CIPD (2014) *Our Minds at Work: Developing the Behavioural Science of HR*. London: CIPD.

Coetzee, V.; Perrett, D.I. and Stephen, I.D. (2009) Facial adiposity: A cue to health? *Perception* 38(11): 1700–1711.

Cohen, A. (2016) Are they among us? A conceptual framework of the relationship between the dark triad personality and counterproductive work behaviors (CWBs). *Human Resource Management Review* 26: 69–85.

Colarelli, S.M. (2003) *No Best Way: An Evolutionary Perspective on Human Resource Management*. Westport: Praeger Publishers.

Cooper, C.L. and Cartwright, S. (1994) Healthy mind; healthy organization: a proactive approach to occupational stress. *Human Relations* 47(4): 455–471.

Couch, K.A. and Fairlie, R. (2010) Last hired, first fired? Black–white unemployment and the business cycle. *Demography* 47(1): 227–247.

Coyne, J.A. (2010) *Why Evolution Is True*. Oxford: Oxford University Press.

Crandal, C.S. (1994) Prejudice against fat people: ideology and self-interest. *Journal of Personality and Social Psychology* 66(5): 882–894.

Crane, D. (2000) *Fashion and its Social Agenda: Class, Gender, and Identity in Clothing*. Chicago: University of Chicago Press.

Crawshaw, L. (2009) Workplace bullying? Mobbing? Harassment? Distraction by a thousand definitions. *Consulting Psychology Journal: Practice and Research*, 61: 263–267.

Cunningham, M.R.; Barbee, A.P. and Pike, C.L. (1990) What do women want? Facialmetric assessment of multiple motives in the perception of male facial physical attractiveness. *Journal of Personality and Social Psychology* 59(1): 61–72.

Cunningham, W.A.; Johnson, M.K.; Raye, C.L.; Gatenby, J.C.; Gore, J.C. and Banaji, M.R. (2004) Separable neural components in the processing of black and white faces. *Psychological Science* 15(12): 806–813.

Curio, E.; Ernst, U. and Vieth, W. (1978) The adaptive significance of avian mobbing. II. Cultural transmission of enemy recognition in blackbirds: effectiveness and some constraints. *Ethology* 48: 184–202.

Daly, M. and Wilson, M. (1988) *Homicide: Foundations of Human Behavior*. New York: Routledge.

Daly, M. and Wilson, M.I. (1999) Human evolutionary psychology and animal behavior. *Animal Behaviour* 57: 509–519.

Darwin, C. ([1859] 1998) *On the Origin of Species*. Ware: Wordsworth.

Darwin, C. ([1871] 2001) *The Descent of Man, and Selection in Relation to Sex*. Princeton: Princeton University Press.

Davis, D. (2009) Transgender issues in the workplace: HRD's newest challenge/opportunity. *Advances in Developing Human Resources* 11(1): 109–120.

Davis, M. (1992) The role of the amygdala in fear and anxiety. *Annual Review of Neuroscience* 15: 353–375.

Davison, H.K. and Burke, M.J. (2000) Sex discrimination in simulated employment contexts: a meta-analytic investigation. *Journal of Vocational Behavior* 56(2): 225–248.

Dawkins, R. (1976) *The Selfish Gene*. Oxford: Oxford University Press.

Dawkins, R. (2006) *The Blind Watchmaker*. London: Penguin.

DeBruine, L.M. (2002) Facial resemblance enhances trust. *Proceedings of the Royal Society of London B: Biological Sciences* 269(1498): 1307–1312.

De Cuyper, N.; Baillien, E. and de Witte, H. (2009) Job insecurity, perceived employability and targets' and perpetrators' experiences of workplace bullying. *Work & Stress* 23: 206–224.

Deitch, E.A.; Barsky, A.; Butz, R.M.; Chan, S.; Brief, A.P. and Bradley, J.C. (2003) Subtle yet significant: the existence and impact of everyday racial discrimination in the workplace. *Human Relations* 56(11): 1299–1324.

Delgado, R. and Stefancic, J. (2017) *Critical Race Theory*. New York: NYU Press.

Devine, P.G. (1989) Stereotypes and prejudice: the automatic and controlled components. *Journal of Personality and Social Psychology* 56(1): 5–18.

Diamond, L.M. and Butterworth, M. (2008) Questioning gender and sexual identity dynamic links over time. *Sex Roles* 59(5/6): 365–376.

Dipboye, R.L. (1990) Laboratory vs. field research in industrial and organizational psychology. *International Review of Industrial and Organizational Psychology* 5: 1–34.

Doan, P.L. (2010) The tyranny of gendered spaces: reflections from beyond the gender dichotomy. *Gender, Place & Culture: A Journal of Feminist Geography* 17(5): 635–654.

Dougherty, D.S. and Hode M.G. (2016) Binary logics and the discursive interpretation of organizational policy: making meaning of sexual harassment policy. *Human Relations* 69(8): 1729–1755.

DuBrin, A.J. (2011) *Impression Management in the Workplace*. New York: Routledge.

Duffy, M. and Sperry, L. (2007) Workplace mobbing: individual and family health consequences. *The Family Journal* 15: 398–404.

Dundon, T. and Rafferty, A. (2018) The (potential) demise of HRM? *Human Resource Management Journal* 28(3): 377–391.

Duntley, J.D. (2005) Adaptations to Dangers from Humans. In *The Handbook of Evolutionary Psychology* (edited by D.M. Buss). Hoboken: John Wiley & Sons, pp. 224–254.

Duntley, J.D. and Buss, D.M. (2011) Homicide adaptations. *Aggression and Violent Behavior* 16: 399–410.

Easteal, P. and Ballard, A.J. (2017) Shutting-up or speaking-up: navigating the invisible line between voice and silence in workplace bullying. *Alternative Law Journal* 42: 47–54.

Easton, A. (1998) Women have deadly desire for paler skin in the Philippines. *The Lancet* 352(9127): 555.

Efe, S.Y and Ayaz, S. (2010) Mobbing against nurses in the workplace in Turkey. *International Nursing Review* 57: 328–334.

Einarsen, S. (2000) Harassment and bullying at work: A review of the Scandinavian approach. *Aggression and Violent Behavior* 5: 371–401.

Einarsen, S. and Skogstad, A. (1996) Bullying at work: epidemiological findings in public and private organizations. *European Journal of Work and Organizational Psychology* 5: 185–201.

Einarsen, S.; Hoel, H. and Notelaers, G. (2009) Measuring exposure to bullying and harassment at work: validity, factor structure and psychometric properties of the Negative Acts Questionnaire—Revised. *Work & Stress* 23: 24–44.

Einarsen, S; Hoel, H.; Zapf, D. and Cooper, C.L. (eds) (2003) *Bullying and Emotional Abuse in the Workplace: International Perspectives in Research and Practice*. London: Taylor & Francis.

Einarsen, S.; Hoel, H.; Zapf, D. and Cooper, C.L. (2011) The Concept of Bullying and Harassment at Work: The European Tradition. In *Bullying and Harassment in the Workplace: Development in Theory, Research, and Practice* (Second edition, edited by S. Einarsen, H. Hoel, D. Zapf and C.L. Cooper). Boca Raton: CRC Press, pp. 3–40.

Espino, R. and Franz, M.M. (2002) Latino phenotypic discrimination revisited: the impact of skin color on occupational status. *Social Science Quarterly* 83(2): 612–623.

Eves, A. (2004) Queer theory, butch/femme identities and lesbian space. *Sexualities* 7(4): 480–496.

Feagin, J.R.; Vera, H. and Batur, P. (2001) *White Racism: The Basics*. New York: Routledge.

Fenstermaker, S. and West, C. (2002) *Doing Gender, Doing Difference: Inequality, Power and Institutional Change*. New York: Routledge.

Fink, B.; Grammer, K. and Thornhill, R. (2001) Human (*Homo sapiens*) facial attractiveness in relation to skin texture and color. *Journal of Comparative Psychology* 115(1): 92–99.

Fink, B.; Neave, N.; Manning, J.T. and Grammer, K. (2006) Facial symmetry and judgements of attractiveness, health and personality. *Personality and Individual Differences* 41: 491–499.

Finkelstein, L.M.; Frautschy Demuth, R.L. and Sweeney, D.L. (2007) Bias against overweight job applicants: further explorations of when and why. *Human Resource Management* 46(2): 203–222.

Fisher, R.J. (1993) Social desirability bias and the validity of indirect questioning. *Journal of Consumer Research* 20(2): 303–315.

Foo, Y.Z.; Simmons, L.W. and Rhodes, G. (2017) Predictors of facial attractiveness and health in humans. *Scientific Reports* 7: 39731.

Forbes Human Resources Council. (2018) Nine strategies to keep unconscious bias out of your HR department. *Forbes*. https://www.forbes.com/sites/forbeshumanresourcescouncil/2018/03/07/nine-strategies-to-keep-unconscious-bias-out-of-your-hr-department/#49c5c1926e53. [Accessed 24 November 2018].

Ford, R.T. (2014) Bias in the air: rethinking employment discrimination law. *Stanford Law Review* 66(6): 1381–1422.

Fox, S. and Cowan, R.L. (2015) Revision of the workplace bullying checklist: the importance of human resource management's role in defining and addressing bullying. *Human Resource Management Journal* 25: 116–130.

Fox, S. and Stallworth, L.E. (2005) Racial/ethnic bullying: exploring links between bullying and racism in the US workplace. *Journal of Vocational Behavior* 66: 438–456.

Freud, S. (2015) *Civilization and its Discontents* (edited by T. Dufresne and translated by G.C. Richter). Peterborough: Broadview Press.

Fruhen, L.S.; Watkins, C.D. and Jones, B.C. (2015) Perceptions of facial dominance, trustworthiness, and attractiveness predict managerial pay awards in experimental tasks. *The Leadership Quarterly* 26(6): 1005–1016.

Gagné, P.; Tewksbury, R. and McGaughey, D. (1997) Coming out and crossing over: identity formation and proclamation in a transgender community. *Gender & Society* 11(4): 478–508.

Garfinkel, H. (2002) *Studies in Ethnomethodology*. Cambridge: Polity Press.

Gatta, M. (2011) In the "Blink" of an Eye: American High-End Small Retail Businesses and the Public Workforce System. In *Retail Work* (edited by I. Grugulis and O. Bozkurt). Basingstoke: Palgrave Macmillan.

Girardi, P.; Monaco, E.; Prestigiacomo, C.; Talamo, A.; Ruberto, A. and Tatarelli, R. (2007) Personality and psychopathological profiles in individuals exposed to mobbing. *Violence and Victims* 22: 172–188.

Glasø, L.; Berge Matthiesen, S.; Birkeland Nielsen, M. and Einarsen, S. (2007) Do targets of workplace bullying portray a general victim personality profile? *Scandinavian Journal of Psychology* 48: 313–319.

Godard, J. (2004) A critical assessment of the high performance paradigm. *British Journal of Industrial Relations* 42(2): 439–478.

Goffman, E. (1959) *The Presentation of Self in Everyday Life*. New York: Anchor.

Goffman, E. (1963) *Stigma: Notes on the Management of Spoiled Identity*. New York: Touchstone.

Golash-Boza, T. (2016) A critical and comprehensive sociological theory of race and racism. *Sociology of Race and Ethnicity* 2(2): 129–141.

Goldsmith, A.H.; Hamilton, D. and Darity, Jr., W. (2006) Shades of discrimination: skin tone and wages. *American Economic Review* 96(2): 242–245.

Gottfredson, L.S. (1997) Why *g* matters: the complexity of everyday life. *Intelligence* 24: 79–132.

Gould, S.J. (1978) Sociobiology: the art of storytelling. *New Scientist* 16: 530–533.

Gould, S.J. (2002) *The Structure of Evolutionary Theory*. Cambridge: Harvard University Press.

Gouvier, W.D.; Sytsma-Jordan, S. and Mayville, S. (2003) Patterns of discrimination in hiring job applicants with disabilities: the role of disability type, job complexity and public contact. *Rehabilitation Psychology* 48: 175–181.

Graham, J.; Nosek, B.A. and Haidt, J. (2012) The moral stereotypes of liberals and conservatives: exaggeration of differences across the political spectrum. *PLoS ONE* 7(12): 1–13.

Grammer, K. and Thornhill, R. (1994) Human (homo sapiens) facial attractiveness and sexual selection: the role of symmetry and averageness. *Journal of Comparative Psychology* 108: 233–242.

Grant, P.R. and Grant, B.R. (2014) *40 Years of Evolution: Darwin's Finches on Daphne Major Island*. Princeton: Princeton University Press.

Graw, B. and Manser, M.B. (2007) The function of mobbing in cooperative meerkats. *Animal Behaviour* 74: 507–517.

Greenhaus, J.H.; Parasuraman, S. and Wormley, W.M. (1990) Effects of race on organizational experiences, job performance evaluations, and career outcomes. *Academy of Management Journal* 33(1): 64–86.

Greenwald, A.G.; McGhee, D.E. and Schwartz, J.L. (1998) Measuring individual differences in implicit cognition: the implicit association test. *Journal of Personality and Social Psychology* 74(6): 1464–1480.

Greenwald, A.G.; Nosek, B.A. and Banaji, M.R. (2003) Understanding and using the implicit association test: I. An improved scoring algorithm. *Journal of Personality and Social Psychology* 85(2): 197–216.

Griesser, M. and Ekman, J. (2005) Nepotistic mobbing behaviour in the Siberian jay, *Perisoreus infaustus*. *Animal Behaviour* 69(2): 345–352.

Grodsky, E. and Pager, D. (2001) The structure of disadvantage: individual and occupational determinants of the black–white wage gap. *American Sociological Review* 66(4): 542–567.

Groeblinghoff, D. and Becker, M. (1996) A case study of mobbing and the clinical treatment of mobbing victims. *European Journal of Work and Organizational Psychology* 5: 277–294.

Guest, D.E. (2011) Human resource management and performance: still searching for some answers. *Human Resource Management Journal* 21(1): 3–13.

Gursky, S. (2005) Predator mobbing in *Tarsius spectrum*. *International Journal of Primatology* 26: 207–221.

Guthrie, J.P. (2001) High-involvement work practices, turnover, and productivity: evidence from New Zealand. *Academy of Management Journal* 44(1): 180–190.

Hackney, K.J. and Perrewé, P.L. (2018) A review of abusive behaviors at work: the development of the process model for studying abuse. *Organizational Psychology Review* 8: 70–92.

Hakim, C. (2011) *Honey Money: The Power of Erotic Capital*. London: Penguin.

Halberstam, J. (1998) *Female Masculinity*. Durham: Duke University Press.

Hall, J.A. and Carter, J.D. (1999) Gender-stereotype accuracy as an individual difference. *Journal of Personality and Social Psychology* 77(2): 350–359.

Hall, R.E. (2006) The bleaching syndrome among people of color: implications of skin color for human behavior in the social environment. *Journal of Human Behavior in the Social Environment* 13(3): 19–31.

Hamermesh, D.S. (2013) *Beauty Pays: Why Attractive People Are More Successful*. Princeton: Princeton University Press.

Hamermesh, D.S. and Biddle, J.E. (1993) Beauty and the Labour Market. NBER Working Paper, No. 4518: 1–29.

Hansen, Å.M.; Hogh, A.; Persson, R.; Karlson, B.; Garde, A.H. and Ørbaek, P. (2006) Bullying at work, health outcomes, and physiological stress response. *Journal of Psychosomatic Research* 60: 63–72.

Harman, G.H. (1965) The inference to the best explanation. *Philosophical Review* 74: 88–95.

Harrison, J.; Grant, J. and Herman, J.L. (2012) A gender not listed here: genderqueers, gender rebels, and otherwise in the National Transgender Discrimination Survey. *LGBTQ Public Policy Journal at the Harvard Kennedy School* 2(1): 13–24.

Hawkins, M. (1997) *Social Darwinism in European and American Thought, 1860–1945*. Cambridge: Cambridge University Press.

Heaphy, E.D. and Dutton, J.E. (2008) Positive social interactions and the human body at work: linking organizations and physiology. *Academy of Management Review* 33(1): 137–162.

Heckman, J.J.; Stixrud, J. and Urzua, S. (2006) The effects of cognitive and noncognitive abilities in labor market outcomes and social behavior. *Journal of Labor Economics* 24: 411–482.

Hill, M.E. (2000) Color differences in the socioeconomic status of African American men: results of a longitudinal study. *Social Forces* 78(4): 1437–1460.

Hodson, R.; Roscigno, V.J. and Lopez, S.H. (2006) Chaos and the abuse of power: workplace bullying in interaction and organizational context. *Work and Occupations* 33: 382–416.

Hoel, H. and Beale, D. (2006) Workplace bullying, psychological perspectives and industrial relations: towards a contextualized and interdisciplinary approach. *British Journal of Industrial Relations* 44: 239–262.

Hoel, H. and Cooper, C. (2000) *Destructive Conflict and Bullying at Work*. Manchester: Manchester School of Management, UMIST.

Hoel, H. and Salin, D. (2003) Organisational Antecedents of Workplace Bullying. In *Bullying and Emotional Abuse in the Workplace: International Perspectives in Research and Practice* (edited by S. Einarsen, H. Hoel, D. Zapf and C.L. Cooper). London: Taylor and Francis, pp. 203–218.

Hoel, H.; Glasø, L.; Hetland, J.; Cooper, C.L. and Einarsen, S. (2010) Leadership styles as predictors of self-reported and observed workplace bullying. *British Journal of Management* 21: 453–468.

Hoel, H.; Sheehan, M.J.; Cooper, C.L. and Einarsen, S. (2011) Organisational Effects of Workplace Bullying. In *Bullying and Emotional Abuse in the Workplace: International Perspectives in Research and Practice* (edited by S. Einarsen, H. Hoel, D. Zapf and C.L. Cooper). London: Taylor and Francis, pp. 129–148.

Hoffman, R.M. and Borders, L.D. (2001) Twenty-five years after the Bem Sex-Role Inventory: a reassessment and new issues regarding classification variability. *Measurement and Evaluation in Counseling and Development* 34(1): 39–55.

Hogg, M.A. (2016) Social Identity Theory. In *Understanding Peace and Conflict Through Social Identity Theory* (edited by S. McKeown, R. Haji and N. Ferguson). Switzerland: Springer International Publishing, pp. 3–17.

Hogg, M.A.; Terry, D.J. and White, K.M. (1995) A tale of two theories: a critical comparison of identity theory with social identity theory. *Social Psychology Quarterly* 58(4): 255–269.

Hogh, A.; Mikkelsen, E.G. and Hansen, A.M. (2011) Individual Consequences of Workplace Bullying/Mobbing. In *Bullying and Harassment in the Workplace: Development in Theory, Research, and Practice* (Second edition, edited by S. Einarsen, H. Hoel, D. Zapf and C.L. Cooper). Boca Raton: CRC Press, pp. 107–128.

Hosoda, M.; Stone-Romero, E.F. and Coats, G. (2003) The effects of physical attractiveness on job-related outcomes: a meta-analysis of experimental studies. *Personnel Psychology* 56(2): 431–462.

Hughes, A.; Trudgill, P. and Watt, D. (2012) *English Accents and Dialects* (Fifth edition). London: Routledge.

Hultin, M. and Szulkin, R. (1999) Wages and unequal access to organizational power: an empirical test of gender discrimination. *Administrative Science Quarterly* 44(3) 453–472.

*Human Resource Management International Digest* (2006). Survival of the fittest: discrimination against obesity in the American workplace. 14(3): 26–28.

Hunter, J.E. and Schmidt, F.L. (1996) Intelligence and job performance: economic and social implications. *Psychology, Public Policy, and Law* 2: 447–472.

Hunter, M.L. (2002) "If you're light you're alright": light skin color as social capital for women of color. *Gender & Society* 16(2): 175–193.

Hunter, M. (2007) The persistent problem of colorism: skin tone, status, and inequality. *Sociology Compass* 1(1): 237–254.

Huselid, M.A. (1995) The impact of human resource management practices on turnover, productivity, and corporate financial performance. *Academy of Management Journal* 38(3): 635–672.

Ichniowski, C.; Shaw, K. and Prennushi, G. (1997) The effects of human resource management practices on productivity: a study of steel finishing lines. *American Economic Review* 87(3): 291–313.

Ilies, R.; Arvey, R.D. and Bouchard, T.J., Jr. (2006) Darwinism, behavioral genetics, and organizational behavior: a review and agenda for future research. *Journal of Organizational Behavior* 27(2): 121–141.

Jackson, S. and Rees, A. (2007) The appalling appeal of nature: the popular influence of evolutionary psychology as a problem for sociology. *Sociology* 41: 917–930.

Jansen, A.S.P.; Nguyen, X.V.; Karpitskiy, V.; Mettenleiter, T.C. and Loewy, A.D. (1995) Central command neurons of the sympathetic nervous system: basis of the fight-or-flight response. *Science* 270: 644–646.

Jenkins, M. (2011) Practice note: is mediation suitable for complaints of workplace bullying? *Conflict Resolution Quarterly* 29: 25–38.

Johnson, S.K.; Podratz, K.E.; Dipboye, R.L. and Gibbons, E. (2010) Physical attractiveness biases in ratings of employment suitability: tracking down the "beauty is beastly" effect. *Journal of Social Psychology* 150: 301–318.

Joinson, A. (1999) Social desirability, anonymity, and Internet-based questionnaires. *Behavior Research Methods, Instruments, & Computers* 31: 433–438.

Jones, A.L. (2018) The influence of shape and colour cue classes on facial health perception. *Evolution and Human Behavior* 39: 19–29.

Jones, A.L.; Porcheron, A.; Sweda, J.R.; Morizot, F. and Russell, R. (2016) Coloration in different areas of facial skin is a cue to health: the role of cheek redness and periorbital luminance in health perception. *Body Image* 17: 57–66.

Jones, B.C.; Little, A.C.; Feinberg, D.R.; Penton-Voak, I.S.; Tiddeman, B.P. and Perrett, D.I. (2004) The relationship between shape symmetry and perceived skin condition in male facial attractiveness. *Evolution and Human Behavior* 25(1): 24–30.

Jones, B.C.; Little, A.C.; Penton-Voak, I.S.; Tiddeman, B.P.; Burt, D.M. and Perrett, D.I. (2001) Facial symmetry and judgements of apparent health: Support for a "good genes" explanation of the attractiveness–symmetry relationship. *Evolution and Human Behavior* 22: 417–429.

Jones, D.; Brace, C.L.; Jankowiak, W.; Laland, K.N. et al. (1995) Sexual selection, physical attractiveness, and facial neoteny: cross-cultural evidence and implications. *Current Anthropology* 36(5): 723–748.

Jones, G. (2010) *Beauty Imagined*. Oxford: Oxford University Press.

Jones, T. (2000) Shades of brown: the law of skin color. *Duke Law Journal* 49: 1487–1557.

Judge, T.A. and Cable, D.M. (2004) The effect of physical height on workplace success and income: preliminary test of a theoretical model. *Journal of Applied Psychology* 89(3): 428–441.

Kalick, S.M.; Zebrowitz, L.A.; Langlois, J.H. and Johnson, R.M. (1998) Does human facial attractiveness honestly advertise health? Longitudinal data on an evolutionary question. *Psychological Science* 9: 8–13.

Kanazawa, S. and Kovar, J.L. (2004) Why beautiful people are more intelligent. *Intelligence* 32: 227–243.

Kant, I. (1951) *Critique of Judgement* (translated and introduced by J.H. Bernard). New York: Hafner Press.

Keashly, L. (1997) Emotional abuse in the workplace: conceptual and empirical issues. *Journal of Emotional Abuse* 1: 85–117.

Keashly, L. and Nowell, B.L. (2003) Conflict, Conflict Resolution and Bullying. In *Bullying and Emotional Abuse in the Workplace* (edited by S. Einarsen, H. Hoel, D. Zapf and C.L. Cooper). London: Taylor and Francis, pp. 339–358.

Ketelaar, T. and Ellis, B.J. (2000) Are evolutionary explanations unfalsifiable? Evolutionary psychology and the Lakatosian philosophy of science. *Psychological Inquiry* 11: 1–21.

King, E.B. and Ahmad, A.S. (2010) An experimental field study of interpersonal discrimination toward Muslim job applicants. *Personnel Psychology* 63(4): 881–906.

Kirkwood, R. and Dickie, J. (2005) Mobbing of a great white shark (*Carcharodon carcharias*) by adult male Australian fur seals (*Arctocephalus pusillus doriferus*). *Marine Mammal Science* 21: 336–339.

Kivimäki, M.; Virtanen, M.; Vartia, M.; Elovainio, M.; Vahtera, J. and Keltikangas-Järvinen, L. (2003) Workplace bullying and the risk of cardiovascular disease and depression. *Occupational and Environmental Medicine* 60: 779–783.

Klesges, R.C.; Klem, M.L.; Hanson, C.L.; Eck, L.H.; Ernst, J.; O'Laughlin, D.; Garrott, A. and Rife, R. (1990) The effects of applicants' health status and qualifications on simulated hiring decisions. *International Journal of Obesity* 14(6): 527–535.

Komarovsky, M. (2004) *The Unemployed Man and His Family.* Walnut Creek: Altamir Press.

Komori, M.; Kawamura, S. and Ishihara, S. (2009) Averageness or symmetry: which is more important for facial attractiveness? *Acta Psychologica* 131: 136–142.

Koser, D.A.; Matsuyama, M. and Kopelman, R.E. (1999) Comparison of physical and mental disability in employee selection: an experimental examination of direct and moderated effects. *North American Journal of Psychology* 1: 213–222.

Kugler, M.; Verdier, T. and Zenou, Y. (2005) Organized crime, corruption, and punishment. *Journal of Public Economics* 89: 1639–1663.

Lamm, C.; Decety, J. and Singer, T. (2011) Meta-analytic evidence for common and distinct neural networks associated with directly experienced pain and empathy for pain. *NeuroImage* 54: 2492–2502.

Lankford, A. (2013) A comparative analysis of suicide terrorists and rampage, workplace, and school shooters in the United States from 1990 to 2010. *Homicide Studies* 17: 255–274.

Larkin, J.C. and Pines, H.A. (1979) No fat persons need apply: experimental studies of the overweight stereotype and hiring preference. *Work and Occupations* 6(3): 312–327.

Lee, A. (2005) Unconscious bias theory in employment discrimination litigation. *Harvard Civil Rights–Civil Liberties Law Review* 40(2): 481–503.

Lee, N.; Senior, C. and Butler, M.J.R. (2012) The domain of organizational cognitive neuroscience: theoretical and empirical challenges. *Journal of Management* 38(4): 921–931.

Lee, S.; Pitesa, M.; Pillutla, M. and Thau, S. (2015) When beauty helps and when it hurts: an organizational context model of attractiveness discrimination in selection decisions. *Organizational Behavior and Human Decision Processes* 128: 15–28.

Lefevre, C.E. and Perrett, D.I. (2015) Fruit over sunbed: carotenoid skin colouration is found more attractive than melanin colouration. *Quarterly Journal of Experimental Psychology* 68(2): 284–293.

Lehmann, E.L. and Romano, J.P. (2005) Generalizations of the familywise error rate. *Annals of Statistics* 33(3): 1138–1154.

Levay, C. (2014) Obesity in organizational context. *Human Relations* 67(5): 565–585.

Lewis, D. and Rayner, C. (2003) Bullying and Human Resource Management: A Wolf in Sheep's Clothing? In *Bullying and Emotional Abuse in the Workplace* (edited by S. Einarsen, H. Hoel, D. Zapf and C.L. Cooper). London: Taylor and Francis, pp. 370–382.

Lewis, M.A. (2006) Nurse bullying: organizational considerations in the maintenance and perpetation of health care bullying cultures. *Journal of Nursing Management*, 14: 52–58.

Leymann, H. (1990) Mobbing and psychological terror at workplaces. *Violence and Victims* 5: 119–126.

Leymann, H. (1996) The content and development of mobbing at work. *European Journal of Work and Organizational Psychology* 5: 165–184.

Leymann, H. and Gustafsson, A. (1996) Mobbing at work and the development of post-traumatic stress disorders. *European Journal of Work and Organizational Psychology* 5: 251–275.

Lindqvist, E. (2012) Height and leadership. *Review of Economics and Statistics* 94(4): 1191–1196.

Linstead, A. and Brewis, J. (2004) Editorial: Beyond boundaries: towards fluidity in theorizing and practice. *Gender, Work & Organization* 11(4): 355–362.

Linstead, S. and Pullen, A. (2006) Gender as multiplicity: desire, displacement, difference and dispersion. *Human Relations* 59(9): 1287–1310.

Lipton, P. (2004) *Inference to the Best Explanation* (Second edition). Routledge: London.

Little, A.C. and Hancock, P.J.B. (2002) The role of masculinity and distinctiveness in judgments of human male facial attractiveness. *British Journal of Psychology* 93(4): 451–464.

Little, A.C.; Burt, D.M.; Penton-Voak, I.S. and Perrett, D.I. (2001) Self-perceived attractiveness influences human female preferences for sexual dimorphism and symmetry in male faces. *Proceedings of the Royal Society B: Biological Sciences* 268: 39–44.

Lopez, S.H.; Hodson, R. and Roscigno, V.J. (2009) Power, status, and abuse at work: general and sexual harassment compared. *The Sociological Quarterly*, 50: 3–27.

Lorber, J. (1994) *Paradoxes of Gender*. New Haven: Yale University Press.

Lorenz, K. (1931) Beiträge zur Ethologie sozialer Corviden. *Journal für Ornithologie* 79: 67–127.

Lorenz, K. (2002) *On Aggression*. London: Routledge.

Lutgen-Sandvik, P. (2008) Intensive remedial identity work: responses to workplace bullying trauma and stigmatization. *Organization* 15: 97–119.

Lutgen-Sandvick, P.; Tracy, S.J. and Alberts, J.K. (2007) Burned by bullying in the American workplace: prevalence, perception, degree, and impact. *Journal of Management Studies* 44: 837–862.

Luxen, M.F. and Van De Vijver, F.J.R. (2006) Facial attractiveness, sexual selection, and personnel selection: when evolved preferences matter. *Journal of Organizational Behavior* 27(2): 241–255.

MacDuffie, J.P. (1995) Human resource bundles and manufacturing performance: organizational logic and flexible production systems in the world auto industry. *Industrial and Labor Relations Review* 48(2): 197–221.

Madera, J.M. and Hebl, M.R. (2012) Discrimination against facially stigmatized applicants in interviews: an eye-tracking and face-to-face investigation. *Journal of Applied Psychology* 97: 317–333.

Mao, J.M.; Haupert, M.L. and Smith, E.R. (2018) How gender identity and transgender status affect perceptions of attractiveness. *Social Psychological and Personality Science* (Online First): 1–12.

Marlowe, C.M.; Schneider, S.L. and Nelson, C.E. (1996) Gender and attractiveness biases in hiring decisions: are more experienced managers less biased? *Journal of Applied Psychology* 81: 11–21.

Marques, J.M. and Paez, D. (1994) The "black sheep effect": social categorization, rejection of ingroup deviates, and perception of group variability. *European Review of Social Psychology* 5: 37–68.

Martin, W. and LaVan, H. (2010) Workplace bullying: a review of litigated cases. *Employee Responsibilities and Rights Journal*, 22: 175–194.

Maslow, A.H. (1943) A theory of human motivation. *Psychological Review* 50: 370–396.

Massey, D.S. and Denton, N.A. (2003) *American Apartheid: Segregation and the Making of the Underclass*. Cambridge: Harvard University Press.

Mataiske, W. (2004) Pourquoi pas? Rational choice as a basic theory of HRM. *Management Revue* 15(2): 249–263.

Matthiesen, S.B. and Einarsen, S. (2001) MMPI-2 configurations among victims of bullying at work. *European Journal of Work and Organizational Psychology* 10: 467–484.

Matts, P.J.; Fink, B.; Grammer, K. and Burquest, M. (2007) Color homogeneity and visual perception of age, health, and attractiveness of female facial skin. *Journal of the American Academy of Dermatology* 57(6): 977–984.

McClelland, G.H. and Judd, C.M. (1993) Statistical difficulties of detecting interactions and moderator effects. *Psychological Bulletin* 114(2): 376–390.

McConnell, A.R. and Leibold, J.M. (2001) Relations among the implicit association test, discriminatory behavior, and explicit measures of racial attitudes. *Journal of Experimental Social Psychology* 37(5): 435–442.

McGinnity, F. and Lunn, P.D. (2011) Measuring discrimination facing ethnic minority job applicants: an Irish experiment. *Work, Employment & Society* 25(4): 693–708.

McLaughlin, H.; Uggen, C. and Blackstone, A. (2012) Sexual harassment, workplace authority, and the paradox of power. *American Sociological Review* 77: 625–647.

Mead, G.H. (1967) *Mind, Self & Society: from the Standpoint of a Social Behaviorist* (edited and introduced by C.W. Morris). Chicago: University of Chicago Press.

Mealey, L.; Bridgstock, R. and Townsend, G.C. (1999) Symmetry and perceived facial attractiveness: a monozygotic co-twin comparison. *Journal of Personality and Social Psychology* 76: 151–158.

Merchant, V. and Hoel, H. (2003) Investigating Complaints of Bullying. In *Bullying and Emotional Abuse in the Workplace* (edited by S. Einarsen, H. Hoel, D. Zapf and C.L. Cooper). London: Taylor and Francis, pp. 259–269.

Mikkelsen, E.G. and Einarsen, S. (2002) Basic assumptions and symptoms of post-traumatic stress among victims of bullying at work. *European Journal of Work and Organizational Psychology* 11: 87–111.

Mishna, F.; Wiener, J. and Pepler, D. (2008) Some of my best friends—experiences of bullying within friendships. *School Psychology International* 29: 549–573.

Moayed, F.A.; Daraiseh, N.; Shell, R. and Sam S. (2006) Workplace bullying: a systematic review of risk factors and outcomes. *Theoretical Issues in Ergonomics Science* 7: 311–327.

Mobius, M.M. and Rosenblat, T.S. (2006) Why beauty matters. *American Economic Review* 96: 222–235.

Mong, S.N. and Roscigno, V.J. (2010) African American men and the experience of employment discrimination. *Qualitative Sociology* 33(1): 1–21.

Morrow, P.C. (1990) Physical attractiveness and selection decision making. *Journal of Management* 16(1): 45–60.

Mugglestone, L. (2007) *Talking Proper: The Rise of Accent as Social Symbol.* Oxford: Oxford University Press.

Mulder, R.; Bos, A.E.R.; Pouwelse, M. and van Dam, K. (2017) Workplace mobbing: how the victim's coping behavior influences bystander responses. *Journal of Social Psychology* 157: 16–29.

Mulder, R.; Pouwelse, M.; Lodewijkx, H. and Bolman, C. (2014) Workplace mobbing and bystanders' helping behaviour towards victims: the role of gender, perceived responsibility and anticipated stigma by association. *International Journal of Psychology* 49: 304–312.

Murphy, G.C. and Athanasou, J.A. (1999) The effect of unemployment on mental health. *Journal of Occupational and Organizational Psychology* 72: 83–99.

Muscarella, F. and Cunningham, M.R. (1996) The evolutionary significance and social perception of male pattern baldness and facial hair. *Ethology and Sociobiology* 17(2): 99–117.

Nadal, K.L.; Whitman, C.N.; Davis, L.S.; Erazo, T. and Davidoff, K.C. (2016) Microaggressions toward lesbian, gay, bisexual, transgender, queer, and queergender people: a review of the literature. *Journal of Sex Research* 53(4/5): 488–508.

Nanda, S. (1999) *Neither Man Nor Woman: The Hijras of India* (Second Edition). Belmont: Wadsworth.

Neal, D. (2004) The measured black–white wage gap among women is too small. *Journal of Political Economy* 112(S1): S1–S28.

Neuman, J.H. and Baron, R.A. (1998) Workplace violence and workplace aggression: evidence concerning specific forms, potential causes, and preferred targets. *Journal of Management* 24: 391–419.

Nguyen, A. (2008) Patriarchy, power, and female masculinity. *Journal of Homosexuality* 55(4): 655–683.

Nicholson, N. (2005) Objections to evolutionary psychology: reflections, implications and the leadership exemplar. *Human Relations* 58(3): 393–409.

Nickson, D.; Timming, A.R.; Re, D. and Perrett, D. (2016) Subtle increases in BMI within a healthy weight range still reduce women's employment chances in the service sector. *PLoS ONE* 11: e0159659.

Nickson, D., Warhurst, C. and Dutton, E. (2005) The importance of attitude and appearance in the service encounter in retail and hospitality. *Managing Service Quality* 15(2): 195–208.

Nickson, D.; Warhurst, C.; Witz, A. and Cullen, A.M. (2001) The Importance of Being Aesthetic: Work, Employment and Service Organization. In *Customer Service* (edited by A. Sturdy, I. Grugulis and H. Willmott). Basingstoke: Palgrave, pp. 170–190.

Nielsen, M.B. and Einarsen, S. (2012) Outcomes of exposure to workplace bullying: a meta-analytic review. *Work and Stress* 26: 309–332.

Nielsen, M.B.; Matthiesen, S.B. and Einarsen, S. (2010) The impact of methodological moderators on prevalence rates of workplace bullying: a meta-analysis. *Journal of Occupational and Organizational Psychology* 83: 955–979.

Nielsen, M.B.; Nielsen, G.H.; Notelaers, G. and Einarsen, S. (2015)

Workplace bullying and suicidal ideation: a 3-wave longitudinal Norwegian study. *American Journal of Public Health* 105: e23–e28.

Nietzsche, F. (2006) *Thus Spoke Zarathustra, A Book for All and None* (edited by A. Del Caro and R.B. Pippin). Cambridge: Cambridge University Press.

Nofal, A.M.; Nicolaou, N.; Symeonidou, N. and Shane, S. (2018) Biology and management: a review, critique, and research agenda. *Journal of Management* 44(1): 7–31.

Nolfe, G.; Petrella, C.; Blasi, F.; Zontini, G. and Nolfe, G. (2007) Psychopathological dimensions of harassment in the workplace (mobbing). *International Journal of Mental Health* 36: 67–85.

Noon, M. (2018) Pointless diversity training: unconscious bias, new racism and agency. *Work, Employment and Society*, 32: 198–209.

Nosek, B.A.; Greenwald, A.G. and Banaji, M.R. (2007) The Implicit Association Test at Age 7: A Methodological and Conceptual Review. In *Automatic Processes in Social Thinking and Behavior* (edited by J.A. Bargh). Hove: Psychology Press.

Novit, M.S. (1981) Genetic screening: new challenge for human resource management? *Human Resource Management* 20(2): 1–8.

Oakes, P. (1996) The Categorization Process: Cognition and the Group in the Social Psychology of Stereotyping. In *Social Groups and Identities: Developing the Legacy of Henri Tajfel* (edited by W.P. Robinson). Oxford: Butterworth Heinemann, pp. 95–120.

Öhman, A. and Mineka, S. (2001) Fears, phobias, and preparedness: toward an evolved module of fear and fear learning. *Psychological Review* 108: 483–522.

Oppenheimer, D.M.; Meyvis, T. and Davidenko, N. (2009) Instructional manipulation checks: detecting satisficing to increase statistical power. *Journal of Experimental Social Psychology* 45(4): 867–872.

Orne, J. (2013) Queers in the line of fire: Goffman's *Stigma* revisited. *The Sociological Quarterly* 54(2): 229–253.

Oxenbridge, S. and Brown, W. (2004) Achieving a new equilibrium? The stability of cooperative employer–union relationships. *Industrial Relations Journal* 35(5): 388–402.

Parker, M. (2002) Queering management and organization. *Gender, Work and Organization* 9(2): 146–166.

Patton, J.H.; Stanford, M.S. and Barratt, E.S. (1995) Factor structure of the Barratt Impulsiveness Scale. *Journal of Clinical Psychology* 51: 768–774.

Paull, M.; Omari, M. and Standen, P. (2012) When is a bystander not a bystander? A typology of the roles of bystanders in workplace bullying. *Asia Pacific Journal of Human Resources* 50: 351–366.

Paustian-Underdahl, S.C. and Slattery Walker, L. (2015) Revisiting the beauty is beastly effect: examining when and why sex and attractiveness impact hiring judgments. *International Journal of Human Resource Management* 27: 1034–1058.

Pavey, C.R. and Smyth, A.K. (1998) Effects of avian mobbing on roost use and diet of powerful owls, *Ninox Strenua*. *Animal Behaviour* 55: 313–318.

Penton-Voak, I.S.; Jones, B.C.; Little, A.C.; Baker, S.; Tiddeman, B.; Burt, D.M. and Perrett, D.I. (2001) Symmetry, sexual dimorphism in facial proportions and male facial attractiveness. *Proceedings of the Royal Society B: Biological Sciences*, 268: 1617–1623.

Perrett, D.I.; Burt, D.M.; Penton-Voak, I.S.; Lee, K.J.; Rowland, D.A. and Edwards, R. (1999) Symmetry and human facial attractiveness. *Evolution and Human Behavior* 20: 295–307.

Perrett, D.I.; Lee, K.J.; Penton-Voak, I.; Rowland, D.; Yoshikawa, S.; Burt, D.M.; Henzi, S.P.; Castles, D.L. and Akamatsu, S. (1998) Effects of sexual dimorphism on facial attractiveness. *Nature* 394: 884–887.

Persico, N.; Postlewaite, A. and Silverman, D. (2004) The effect of adolescent experience on labor market outcomes: the case of height. *Journal of Political Economy* 112(5): 1019–1053.

Peterson, R.B. and Lewin, D. (2000) Research on unionized grievance procedures: management issues and recommendations. *Human Resource Management*, 39: 395–406.

Pettifor, R.A. (1990) The effects of avian mobbing on a potential predator, the European kestrel, *Falco tinnunculus*. *Animal Behaviour* 39: 821–827.

Pettinger, L. (2004) Brand culture and branded workers: service work and aesthetic labour in fashion retail. *Consumption, Markets & Culture* 7: 165–184.

Pezdirc, K.; Rolla, M.E.; Whitehead, R.; Hutchesson, M.J.; Ozakinci, G.; Perrett, D. and Collins, C.E. (2018) Perceptions of carotenoid and melanin coloration in faces among young Australian adults. *Australian Journal of Psychology* 70(1): 85–90.

Pfeffer, J. (1994) *Competitive Advantage Through People: Unleashing the Power of the Work Force*. Boston: Harvard Business School Press.

Phelps, E.A.; O'Connor, K.J.; Cunningham, W.A.; Funayama, E.S.;

Gatenby, J.C.; Gore, J.C. and Banaji, M.R. (2000) Performance on indirect measures of race evaluation predicts amygdala activation. *Journal of Cognitive Neuroscience* 12(5): 729–738.

Pilch, I. and Turska, E. (2015) Relationships between Machiavellianism, organizational culture, and workplace bullying: emotional abuse from the target's and the perpetrator's perspective. *Journal of Business Ethics* 128: 83–93.

Pingitore, R.; Dugoni, B.L.; Tindale, R.S. and Spring, B. (1994) Bias against overweight job applicants in a simulated employment interview. *Journal of Applied Psychology* 79(6): 909–917.

Pound, N.; Lawson, D.W.; Toma, A.M.; Richmond, S.; Zhurov, A.I. and Penton-Voak, I.S. (2014) Facial fluctuating asymmetry is not associated with childhood ill-health in a large British cohort study. *Proceedings of the Royal Society B: Biological Sciences* 281: 1–7.

Prasad, A. (2012) Beyond analytical dichotomies. *Human Relations* 65(5): 567–595.

Presti, D.E. (2016) *Foundational Concepts in Neuroscience: A Brain–Mind Odyssey*. New York: W.W. Norton & Company.

Prokosch, M.D.; Yeo, R.A. and Miller, G.F. (2005) Intelligence tests with higher g-loadings show higher correlations with body symmetry: evidence for a general fitness factor mediated by developmental stability. *Intelligence* 33: 203–213.

Quillian, L. (2008) Does unconscious racism exist? *Social Psychology Quarterly* 71(1): 6–11.

Quine, L. (1999) Workplace bullying in NHS community trust: staff questionnaire survey. *BMJ* 318: 228–231.

Rantala, M.J.; Coetzee, V.; Moore, F.R.; Skrinda, I.; Kecko, S.; Krama, T.; Kivleniece, I. and Krams, I. (2013) Adiposity, compared with masculinity, serves as a more valid cue to immunocompetence in human mate choice. *Proceedings of the Royal Society B: Biological Sciences* 280(1751): 20122495.

Rayner, C. (1997) The incidence of workplace bullying. *Journal of Community & Applied Social Psychology* 7: 199–208.

Rayner, C. and Hoel, H. (1997) A summary review of literature relating to workplace bullying. *Journal of Community & Applied Social Psychology* 7: 181–191.

Rayner, C.; Sheehan, M. and Barker, M. (1999) Theoretical approaches to the study of bullying at work. *International Journal of Manpower* 20: 11–16.

Re, D.; Whitehead, R.D.; Xiao, D. and Perrett, D.I. (2011) Oxygenated-blood colour change thresholds for perceived facial redness, health, and attractiveness. *PLoS ONE* 6(3): e17859.

Reddy, G. (2010) *With Respect to Sex: Negotiating Hijra Identity in South India.* Chicago: University of Chicago Press.

Rees, D.C.; Williams, T.N. and Gladwin, M.T. (2010) Sickle-cell disease. *The Lancet* 376(9757): 2018–2031.

Reik, B.M.; Mania, E.W. and Gaertner, S.L. (2006) Intergroup threat and outgroup attitudes: a meta-analytic review. *Personality and Social Psychology Review* 10(4): 336–353.

Rhodes, G. (2006) The evolutionary psychology of facial beauty. *Annual Review of Psychology* 57: 199–226.

Rhodes, G.; Hickford, C. and Jeffrey, L. (2000) Sex typicality and attractiveness: are supermale and superfemale faces super attractive? *British Journal of Psychology* 91(1): 125–140.

Rhodes, G.; Proffitt, F.; Grady, J.M. and Sumich, A. (1998) Facial symmetry and the perception of beauty. *Psychonomic Bulletin and Review* 5: 659–669.

Rhodes, G.; Yoshikawa, S.; Palermo, R.; Simmons, L.W.; Peters, M.; Lee, K.; Halberstadt, J. and Crawford, J.R. (2007) *Perception* 36(8): 1244–1252.

Rhodes, G.; Yoshikawa, S.; Clark, A.; Lee, K.; McKay, R. and Akamatsu, S. (2001a) Attractiveness of facial averageness and symmetry in non-western cultures: in search of biologically based standards of beauty. *Perception*, 30: 611–625.

Rhodes, G.; Zebrowitz, L.A.; Clark, A.; Kalick, S.M.; Hightower, A. and McKay, R. (2001b) Do facial averageness and symmetry signal health? *Evolution and Human Behavior* 22: 31–46.

Richards, C.; Bouman, W.P.; Seal, L.; Barker, M.J.; Nieder, T.O. and T'Sjoen, G. (2016) Non-binary or genderqueer genders. *International Review of Psychiatry* 28(1): 95–102.

Richeson, J.A.; Baird, A.A.; Gordon, H.L.; Heatherton, T.F.; Wyland, C.L.; Trawalter, S. and Shelton, J.N. (2003) An fMRI investigation of the impact of interracial contact on executive function. *Nature Neuroscience* 6: 1323–1328.

Ridley, M. (2003) *The Agile Gene: How Nature Turns on Nurture.* New York: Harper Collins.

Robinson, S.L.; O'Reilly, J. and Wang, W. (2013) Invisible at work: an integrated model of workplace ostracism. *Journal of Management* 39: 203–231.

Rockquemore, K.A.; Brunsma, D.L. and Delgado, D.J. (2009) Racing to theory or retheorizing race? Understanding the struggle to build a multiracial identity theory. *Journal of Social Issues* 65(1): 13–34.

Rooth, D.O. (2007) Implicit Discrimination in Hiring: Real World Evidence. IZA Discussion Paper Series No. 2764.

Rousseau, J.J. (2013) *The Social Contract* (translated by H.J. Tozer and introduced by D. Matravers). Ware: Wordsworth.

Rubin, H. (2003) *Self-Made Men: Identity and Embodiment among Transsexual Men.* Nashville: Vanderbilt University Press.

Rudolph, C.W.; Wells, C.L.; Weller, M.D. and Baltes, B.B. (2009) A meta-analysis of empirical studies of weight-based bias in the workplace. *Journal of Vocational Behavior* 74: 1–10.

Ruggs, E.N.; Hebl, M.R. and Williams, A. (2015) Weight isn't selling: the insidious effects of weight stigmatization in retail settings. *Journal of Applied Psychology* 100(5): 1483–1496.

Ryan, C.S. (1996) Accuracy of black and white college students' in-group and out-group stereotypes. *Personality and Social Psychology Bulletin* 22(11): 1114–1127.

Saad, G. (2007) *The Evolutionary Bases of Consumption.* Mahway: Lawrence Erlbaum.

Saad, G. (2011) *The Consuming Instinct: What Juicy Burgers, Ferraris, Pornography, and Gift Giving Reveal about Human Nature.* Amhurst: Prometheus.

Salin, D. (2001) Prevalence and forms of bullying among business professionals: a comparison of two different strategies for measuring bullying. *European Journal of Work and Organizational Psychology* 10: 425–441.

Salin, D. (2003) Ways of explaining workplace bullying: a review of enabling, motivating, and precipitating structures and processes in the work environment. *Human Relations* 56: 1213–1232.

Sayer, A. (2007) Dignity at work: broadening the agenda. *Organization* 14: 565–581.

Scheib, J.E.; Gangestad, S.W. and Thornhill, R. (1999) Facial attractiveness, symmetry and cues of good genes. *Proceedings of the Royal Society of London B: Biological Sciences* 266: 1913–1917.

Schmidt, F.L. and Hunter, J.E. (1998) The validity and utility of selection methods in personnel psychology: practical and theoretical implications of 85 years of research findings. *Psychological Bulletin* 124: 262–274.

Schultz, T.P. (2002) Wage gains associated with height as a form of health human capital. *American Economic Review* 92(2): 349–353.

Schutz, A. (1967) *The Phenomenology of the Social World*. Evanston: Northwestern University Press.

Schwartz, M.B.; O'Neal Chambliss, H.; Browness, K.D.; Blair, S.N. and Billington, C. (2003) Weight bias among health professionals specializing in obesity. *Obesity Research* 11(9): 1033–1039.

Scott-Phillips, P., Thomas C.; Dickins, T.E. and Stuart A.W. (2011) Evolutionary theory and the ultimate-proximate distinction in the human behavioral sciences. *Perspectives on Psychological Science* 6: 38–47.

Sewell, G. (2004) Yabba-dabba-doo! Evolutionary psychology and the rise of Flintstone psychological thinking in organization and management studies. *Human Relations* 57(8): 923–955.

Shackelford, T.K. and Larsen, R.J. (1999) Facial attractiveness and physical health.*Evolution and Human Behavior* 20: 71–76.

Shallcross, L.; Sheehan, M. and Ramsay, S. (2008) Workplace mobbing: experiences in the public sector. *International Journal of Organisational Behaviour* 13: 56–70.

Sherif, M. (2015) *Group Conflict and Co-operation: Their Social Psychology*. London: Psychology Press.

Simmons, L.W. (2005) The evolution of polyandry: sperm competition, sperm selection and offspring viability. *Annual Review of Ecology, Evolution, and Systematics* 36: 125–146.

Singh, D. and Young, R.K. (1995) Body weight, waist-to-hip ratio, breasts, and hips: role in judgments of female attractiveness and desirability for relationships. *Ethology and Sociobiology* 16(6): 483–507.

Skarlicki, D.P. and Folger, R. (1997) Retaliation in the workplace: the roles of distributive, procedural, and interactional justice. *Journal of Applied Psychology* 82: 434–443.

Slominski, A.; Tobin, D.J.; Shibahara, S. and Wortsman, J. (2004) Melanin pigmentation in mammalian skin and its hormonal regulation. *Physiological Reviews* 84(4): 1155–1228.

Smith, K.L.; Cornellisen, P.L. and Tovee, M.J. (2007) Color 3D bodies and judgements of human female attractiveness. *Evolution and Human Behavior* 28(1): 48–54.

Smith, R.L. (ed.) (1984) *Sperm Competition and the Evolution of Animal Mating Systems*. Orlando: Academic Press.

Smyth, R.; Jacobs, G. and Rogers, H. (2003) Male voices and perceived sexual orientation: an experimental and theoretical approach. *Language in Society* 32(3): 329–350.

Spector, P.E.; Coulter, M.L.; Stockwell, H.G. and Matz, M.W. (2007) Perceived violence climate: a new construct and its relationship to workplace physical violence and verbal aggression, and their potential consequences. *Work & Stress* 21: 117–130.

Spencer, H. (1884) *The Principles of Biology*. London: Williams & Norgate.

Stephen, I.D.; Coetzee, V.; Smith, M.L and Perrett, D.I. (2009a) Skin blood perfusion and oxygenation colour affect perceived human health. *PLoS ONE*, 4: e5083.

Stephen, I.D.; Law Smith, M.J.; Stirrat, M.R. and Perrett, D.I. (2009b) Facial skin coloration affects perceived health of human faces. *International Journal of Primatology* 30(6): 845–857.

Stephen, I.D.; Scott, I.M.L.; Coetzee, V.; Pound, N.; Perrett, D.I. and Penton-Voak, I.S. (2012) Cross-cultural effects of color, but not morphological masculinity, on perceived attractiveness of men's faces. *Evolution and Human Behavior* 33(4): 260–267.

Sumerau, J.E.; Mathers, L.A.B.; Nowakowski, A.C.H. and Cragun, R.T. (2017) Helping quantitative sociology come out of the closet. *Sexualities* 20(5–6): 644–656.

Sumner, W.G. (1940) *Folkways—A Study of the Sociological Importance of Usages, Manners, Customs, Mores and Morals*. Boston: Ginn & Co.

Swami, V.; Rozmus-Wrzesinska, M.; Voracek, M.; Haubner, T.; Danel, D. et al. (2008) The influence of skin tone, body weight, and hair colour on perceptions of women's attractiveness and health: a cross-cultural investigation. *Journal of Evolutionary Psychology* 6(4): 321–341.

Swann Jr., W.B.; Jetten, J.; Gómez, Á.; Whitehouse, H. and Brock, B. (2012) When group membership gets personal: a theory of identity fusion. *Psychological Review* 119(3): 441–456.

Szymanski, D.M.; Moffitt, L.B. and Carr, E.R. (2011) Sexual objectification of women: advances to theory and research. *The Counseling Psychologist* 39(1): 6–38.

Tajfel, H. (1957) Value and the perceptual judgement of magnitude. *Psychological Review* 64(3): 192–204.

Tajfel, H. (1981) *Human Groups and Social Categories: Studies in Social Psychology*. Cambridge: Cambridge University Press.

Tajfel, H. (1982) Social psychology of intergroup relations. *Annual Review of Psychology*. 33(1): 1–39.

Tajfel, H. (ed.) (2010) *Social Identity and Intergroup Relations*. Cambridge: Cambridge University Press.

Tajfel, H. and Turner, J.C. (2004) The Social Identity Theory of Intergroup Behavior. In *Political Psychology: Key Readings* (edited by J.T. Jost and J. Sidanius). New York: Psychology Press, pp. 276–293.

Tajfel, H. and Wilkes, A.L. (1963) Classification and quantitative judgement. *British Journal of Psychology* 54(2): 101–114.

Tepper, B.J. (2007) Abusive supervision and work organizations: review, synthesis, and research agenda. *Journal of Management* 33: 261–289.

Tews, M.J.; Stafford, K. and Zhu, J. (2009) Beauty revisited: the impact of attractiveness, ability, and personality in the assessment of employment suitability. *International Journal of Selection and Assessment* 17(1): 92–100.

Thornhill, R. and Gangestad, S.W. (2006) Facial sexual dimorphism, developmental stability, and susceptibility to disease in men and women. *Evolution and Human Behavior* 27: 131–144.

Timming, A.R. (2010) Dissonant cognitions in European works councils: a "comparative Ethnomethodological" approach. *Economic and Industrial Democracy* 31(4): 521–535.

Timming, A.R. (2015) Visible tattoos in the service sector: a new challenge to recruitment and selection. *Work, Employment & Society*, 29(1): 60–78.

Timming, A.R. (2016) Aesthetic Labour. In *Encyclopaedia of Human Resource Management* (edited by A. Wilkinson and S. Johnstone). Cheltenham, U.K. and Northampton, M.A., U.S.A.: Edward Elgar, pp. 7–8.

Timming, A.R. (2017a) Body art as branded labour: At the intersection of employee selection and relationship marketing. *Human Relations* 70(9): 1041–1063.

Timming, A.R. (2017b) The effect of foreign accent on employability: a study of the aural dimensions of aesthetic labour in customer-facing and non-customer-facing jobs. *Work, Employment & Society* 31(3): 409–428.

Timming, A.R. and Johnstone, S. (2015) Employee silence and the authoritarian personality: a political psychology of workplace democracy. *International Journal of Organizational Analysis* 23(1): 154–171.

Timming, A.R. and Perrett, D.I. (2016) Trust and mixed signals: a study of religion, tattoos and cognitive dissonance. *Personality and Individual Differences* 97: 234–238.

Timming, A.R. and Perrett, D.I. (2017) An experimental study of the effects of tattoo genre on perceived trustworthiness: Not all tattoos are created equal. *Journal of Trust Research* 7(2): 115–128.

Timming, A.R.; Nickson, D.; Re, D. and Perrett, D. (2017) What do you think of my ink? Assessing the effects of body art on employment chances. *Human Resource Management* 56(1): 133–149.

Tracy, S.J.; Lutgen-Sandvik, P. and Alberts, J.K. (2006) Nightmares, demons, and slaves: exploring the painful metaphors of workplace bullying. *Management Communication Quarterly* 20: 148–185.

Trivers, R.L. (1971) The evolution of reciprocal altruism. *The Quarterly Review of Biology* 46(1): 35–57.

Turner, J.C.; Hogg, M.A.; Oakes, P.J.; Reicher, S.D. and Wetherell, M.S. (1987) *Rediscovering the Social Group: A Self-Categorization Theory*. New York: Basil Blackwell.

Vandekerckhove, W. and Commers, M.S.R. (2003) Downward workplace mobbing: a sign of the times? *Journal of Business Ethics* 45: 41–50.

Vartia, M.; Korppoo, L.; Fallenius, S. and Mattila, M.L. (2003) Workplace Bullying: The Role of Occupational Health Services. In *Bullying and Emotional Abuse in the Workplace* (edited by S. Einarsen, H. Hoel, D. Zapf and C.L. Cooper). London: Taylor and Francis, pp. 285–298.

Veblen, T. (1925) *The Theory of the Leisure Class*. London: George Allen & Unwin.

Wadsworth, M.E.J.; Montgomery, S.M. and Bartley, M.J. (1999) The persisting effect of unemployment on health and social well-being in men early in working life. *Social Science & Medicine*, 48: 1491–1499.

Waitt, C.; Little, A.C.; Wolfensohn, S.; Honess, P.; Brown, A.P.; Buchanan-Smith, H.M. and Perrett, D.I. (2003) Evidence from rhesus macaques suggests that male coloration plays a role in female primate mate choice. *Proceedings of the Royal Society of London B: Biological Sciences* 270(Suppl 2): S144–S146.

Walby, S. (1990) *Theorizing Patriarchy*. Oxford: Basil Blackwell.

Warhurst, C. (2016) From Invisible Work to Invisible Workers: The Impact of Service Employers' Speech Demands on the Working Class. In *Invisible Labor: Hidden Work in the Contemporary*

*World* (edited by M. Crain, W. Poster and M. Cherry). Oakland: University of California Press.

Warhurst, C. and Nickson, D. (2007) Employee experience of aesthetic labour in retail and hospitality. *Work, Employment & Society* 21: 103–120.

Warhurst, C. and Nickson, D. (2009) "Who's got the look?" Emotional, aesthetic and sexualized labour interactive services. *Gender, Work & Organization* 16: 385–404.

Warhurst, C.; Nickson, D.; Witz, A. and Cullen, A.M. (2000) Aesthetic labour in interactive service work: some case study evidence from the "new" Glasgow. *Service Industries Journal* 20: 1–18.

Warhurst, C.; van den Broek, D.; Hall, R. and Nickson, D. (2009) Lookism: the new frontier of employment discrimination. *Journal of Industrial Relations*, 51: 131–136.

Weichselbaumer, D. and Winter-Ember, R. (2005) A meta-analysis of the international gender wage gap. *Journal of Economic Surveys* 19(3): 479–511.

West, C. and Zimmerman, D. (1987) Doing gender. *Gender & Society* 1(2): 125–151.

West, S.A.; Griffin, A.S.; Gardner, A. and Diggle, S.P. (2006) Social evolution theory for microorganisms. *Nature Reviews Microbiology* 4: 597–607.

White, R.E.; Thornhill, S. and Hampson, E. (2006) Entrepreneurs and evolutionary biology: the relationship between testosterone and new venture creation. *Organizational Behavior and Human Decision Processes* 100(1): 21–34.

Whitehead, N.L. (2004). On the Poetics of Violence. In *Violence* (edited by N.L. Whitehead). Santa Fe: School of American Research.

Williams, G.C. (2008) *Adaptation and Natural Selection: A Critique of Some Current Evolutionary Thought*. Princeton: Princeton University Press.

Willness, C.R.; Steel, P. and Lee, K. (2007) A meta-analysis of the antecedents and consequences of workplace sexual harassment. *Personnel Psychology* 60: 127–162.

Wilson, E.O. (1975) *Sociobiology: The New Synthesis*. Cambridge: Harvard University Press.

Wilson, W.J. (1997) *When Work Disappears: The World of the New Urban Poor*. New York: Vintage.

Wolf, N. (1991) *The Beauty Myth: How Images of Beauty Are Used Against Women*. London: Vintage.

Wood, S. (1999) Human resource management and performance. *International Journal of Management Reviews* 1(4): 367–413.

Woodrow, C. and Guest, D.E. (2014) When good HR gets bad results: exploring the challenge of HR implementation in the case of workplace bullying. *Human Resource Management Journal* 24: 38–56.

Wright, T.A. and Diamond, W.J. (2006) Getting the "pulse" of your employees: the use of cardiovascular research in better understanding behavior in organizations. *Journal of Organizational Behavior* 27(3): 395–401.

Wyss, S.E. (2004) "This was my hell": the violence experienced by gender non-conforming youth in US high schools. *International Journal of Qualitative Studies in Education* 17(5): 709–730.

Zaidel, D.W.; Aarde, S.M. and Baig, K. (2005) Appearance of symmetry, beauty and health in human faces. *Brain and Cognition* 57: 261–263.

Zapf, D. (1999) Organisational, group work related and personal causes of mobbing/bullying at work. *International Journal of Manpower* 20: 70–85.

Zapf, D. and Einarsen, S. (2003) Individual Antecedents of Bullying: Victims and Perpetrators. In *Bullying and Emotional Abuse in the Workplace* (edited by S. Einarsen, H. Hoel, D. Zapf and C.L. Cooper). London: Taylor and Francis, pp. 165–184.

Zapf, D. and Einarsen, S. (2005) Mobbing at Work: Escalated Conflicts in Organizations. In *Counterproductive Work Behavior: Investigations of Actors and Targets* (edited by S. Fox and P.E. Spector). Washington, D.C.: APA, pp. 237–270.

Zapf, D. and Gross, C. (2001) Conflict escalation and coping with workplace bullying: A replication and extension. *European Journal of Work and Organizational Psychology* 10: 497–522.

Zebrowitz, L.A.; Hall, J.A.; Murphy, N.A. and Rhodes, G. (2002) Looking smart and looking good: facial cues to intelligence and their origins. *Personality and Social Psychology Bulletin* 28: 238–249.

Zimbardo, P. (2007) *The Lucifer Effect*. New York: Random House.